Towns and Villages
OF ENGLAND

STOW-ON-
THE-WOLD

J O A N   J O H N S O N

ALAN SUTTON

First published in the United Kingdom in 1994
Alan Sutton Publishing Ltd · Phoenix Mill · Far Thrupp · Stroud · Gloucestershire

First published in the United States of America in 1994
Alan Sutton Publishing Inc. · 83 Washington Street · Dover · NH 03820

British Library Cataloguing-in-Publication Data

A catalogue record for this book is available from the British Library.

ISBN 0–7509–0590–5

Library of Congress Cataloging-in-Publication Data applied for.

Typeset in 11/13 Bembo.
Typesetting and origination by
Alan Sutton Publishing Limited.
Printed in Great Britain by
Hartnolls Ltd, Bodmin, Cornwall.

Contents

STOW -on-the- WOLD

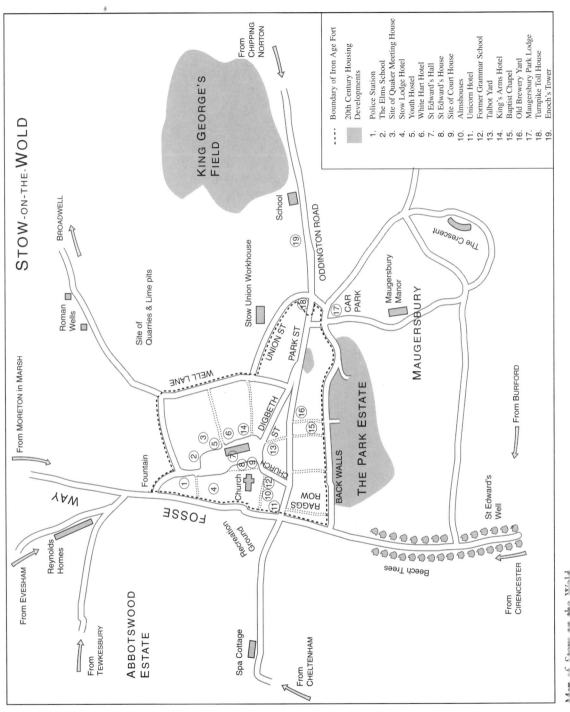

Legend:
- – – – – Boundary of Iron Age Fort
- ▨ 20th Century Housing Developments

1. Police Station
2. The Elms School
3. Site of Quaker Meeting House
4. Stow Lodge Hotel
5. Youth Hostel
6. White Hart Hotel
7. St Edward's Hall
8. St Edward's House
9. Site of Court House
10. Almshouses
11. Unicorn Hotel
12. Former Grammar School
13. Talbot Yard
14. King's Arms Hotel
15. Baptist Chapel
16. Old Brewery Yard
17. Maugersbury Park Lodge
18. Turnpike Toll House
19. Enoch's Tower

KING GEORGE'S FIELD

From CHIPPING NORTON

BROADWELL

Roman Wells

Site of Quarries & Lime pits

From MORETON in MARSH

WELL LANE

Fountain

FOSSE WAY

From EVESHAM

Reynolds Homes

ABBOTSWOOD ESTATE

From TEWKESBURY

Recreation Ground

Spa Cottage

From CHELTENHAM

Church

DIGBETH ST

CHURCH ST

RAGGS ROW

BACK WALLS

THE PARK ESTATE

UNION ST

PARK ST

Stow Union Workhouse

School

ODDINGTON ROAD

CAR PARK

Maugersbury Manor

The Crescent

MAUGERSBURY

From BURFORD

St Edward's Well

Beech Trees

From CIRENCESTER

Map of Stow-on-the-Wold

CHAPTER ONE

From Hut Village to Rural Market

'Stow-on-the-Wold where the wind blows cold and the cooks can't roast their dinners' is a well-known rhyme, but one that gives a misleading impression of a place which, far from being bleak and inhospitable, has attracted successive groups of settlers and has been continually occupied since Neolithic times because of clearly recognized advantages: the security of its elevated position; a supply of water at the spring-line on the side of the hill; workable land for farming; and, most important of all, accessibility from the north and south along the Cotswold Hills and from the Thames and Severn valleys to the east and west of the watershed.

The earliest evidence of habitation here is of Neolithic people who moved into the area from the direction of the Bristol Channel in search of places where they could hunt and fish and grow their own food. Their houses and means of cultivation were primitive, but they were skilled workers in flint from which they fashioned tools and weapons. They were also able to work in stone because long barrows, used for burial, found near Stow were elaborately constructed of quarried stone, and must have needed skilled and organized labour to build.

The most interesting feature of the Neolithic settlement, in view of Stow's later development, is that the inhabitants engaged in trade. Proof of this comes from the ground and polished stone axes found locally, which came from a factory in North Wales. These must have been brought to the area by traders journeying along the Cotswold Way through Stow, and bartered in exchange for any surplus goods that local people had to offer.

Trade continued to play an important part in the lives of the next settlers at Stow, Bronze Age people who infiltrated the area from the Thames Valley, *c.* 2000 BC. They were subsistence farmers like their predecessors, but also knew about bronze and gold and how to use them. From Cornwall and Wales they obtained ingots of tin and copper which smiths fashioned into goods to satisfy local demands; and gold was brought to the area from Ireland and made into ornaments and jewellery. As barter was still the chief means of acquiring whatever was needed or wanted, farming must have been successful enough to produce a considerable surplus of grain, skins and wool to offer in exchange for the coveted ores.

Axe heads found in the Stow area

Evidence of Bronze Age settlement in the Stow area survives in the round burial mounds found among the Neolithic long barrows at Lower Swell, and in the stone circles built for religious purposes at Great Rollright and Cornwell. The first, still well preserved, resembles the larger and better-known circles at Stonehenge and Avebury; the latter, a formation of four rings and a detached monolith, has now largely disappeared. All indicate that at least in respect of religion there was communal activity among these people.

So far, the settlement at Stow had been a vaguely defined collection of huts and small plots on the east side of the hill, with a certain amount of mobility both within and outside the village as flimsy dwellings were replaced by newer ones, and tired land abandoned in favour of more productive sites. With the arrival of the next settlers, Iron Age people (*c.* 800 BC), a noticeable change took place, as these men were more advanced technologically and able to farm on a larger scale than their predecessors; they also preferred to live in well-defined and protected settlements. At Stow they built one of their typical hill-forts, with earth ramparts and a ditch enclosing a considerable area, the boundaries running approximately north–south along the line of the present

Stone circle at Great Rollright

Fosse Way; east along Back Walls in the direction of Maugersbury; then north towards the Broadwell springs and west to rejoin the line of the Fosse. The community was now spreading from its original nucleus along the spring-line towards the top of the hill, and occupied an area large enough to include houses, workshops, storage areas and pens for animals. It was probably at this time that the earliest name for Stow (Maugersbury) was coined in the Celtic tongue used by its inhabitants – 'Maethelgeres Byrig' – the *stronghold of Maethelgar* who was evidently an important personage in the settlement.

As well as being successful farmers, the Iron Age inhabitants of Stow were skilful craftsmen capable of producing pottery and objects of good quality in wood and metal. They carried on trade with the continent and other parts of Britain and facilitated their business transactions by using, as a kind of currency, iron bars that resembled half-formed swords and may indeed have been turned into weapons on occasion. Their peaceful and prosperous existence continued until about 100 BC when it was threatened by the arrival of a more forceful and aggressive Belgic tribe – the Dubonni – bent on acquiring land for their own use. More and stronger forts were built as a defence against the invaders, one only a few miles from Stow at Salmonsbury, but they were not adequate to withstand the superior numbers and strategy of the newcomers who proceeded to move into the whole of the Cotswold area, establishing a new capital settlement at Bagendon, near Cirencester, whence they dominated the surrounding countryside and exercised an economic and cultural influence over its inhabitants.

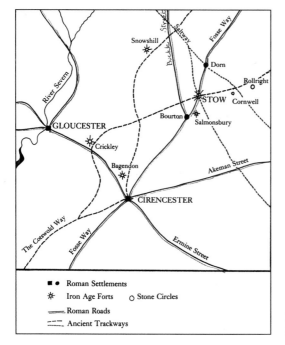

Early tracks and settlements round Stow

However unpopular their arrival in the first place, the presence of the Dubonni in the Cotswolds proved a blessing when the next invasion occurred. The coming of the Romans under Julius Caesar in 55 BC scarcely affected the western part of Britain at all, but the conquest and occupation of the whole country which followed the landing of Claudius in AD 43 might well have led to widespread bloodshed and the imposition of military rule in Gloucestershire had not the Dubonni, very early on, come to terms with the invaders and accepted them as allies rather than conquerors, thus establishing a relationship of great mutual advantage. The Romans were saved from having to keep large garrisons in the Cotswold area to subdue it; the Dubonni were afforded protection by the Romans while being left free to conduct their domestic affairs as they had done before.

Although in a sense Gloucestershire was a frontier area in Roman Britain, since beyond the Severn were Celtic tribes as yet unsubdued and therefore dangerous, nevertheless it was not treated as a military zone but rather as a region where what the Romans considered as civilized life should and could be achieved. The chief means whereby they spread their ideas and standards were the roads, which they built to facilitate the safe and rapid movement of troops, civilians and goods throughout the area between the Thames and the Severn. The centre of communications in the Cotswold area was Cirencester, whence new roads were constructed to radiate in all directions; and for Stow the most important of these was the Fosse Way, designed to run straight along the top of the hills, a more direct route to the Midlands than that of the Cotswold Way which had kept to the lower western slopes of the escarpment. Now it was the Fosse, rather than the older track, which carried the bulk of trade and travellers through the region – wagons, carts, packhorses and itinerant pedlars bearing goods to Cirencester to be rendered as dues or sold in the market, and returning loaded with basic necessities and imported luxury goods. Along the Fosse Way at regular intervals, posting stations were set up to provide accommodation and facilities for travellers – inns, smithies and stabling; Stow was situated between two of these – at Bourton-on-the-Water and Dorn – and no doubt provided an extra stopping place for those passing by on the road, and a useful alternative market to Cirencester.

Presently, also on the Fosse Way or at any rate within easy reach of it, appeared villas, another characteristic feature of the Roman occupation. These varied considerably in size and significance, from luxurious country houses surrounded by vast estates run by dependent labourers like the elaborate establishment at Chedworth, to the modest farmhouses worked by family groups like those found in the neighbourhood of Stow. The owners of the latter were probably local men of limited means but sufficient ambition and enterprise to emulate the Roman way of life by moving outside the bounds of the hill-fort and providing themselves with a more elaborate establishment than they had had previously. Whether they lived within the confines of the settlement or outside,

Roman well at Stow

the day to day routine of the people of Stow would have been little changed under Roman rule. Arable farming combined with stock rearing continued to be the basic pattern with an increased emphasis on the keeping of cattle as draught animals and for their hides, horn and bone rather than for meat. Dogs for hunting and horses for military use were bred in increased numbers; also large herds of sheep and goats for their wool and fleeces.

Locally, woollen cloth was already being woven and worn in the Bronze Age and had become a profitable item of trade, so that even before the arrival of the Romans, British woollen goods were known in Europe. Now they were to become a major export, waterproof cloaks of goat's wool and blankets of sheep's wool being greatly in demand; and the processing of wool into cloth, hitherto an established feature of farmhouse life in the area, was expanded to meet the need for increased supplies. Roman influences were effectively turning a domestic ploy into a business and preparing the way for the staple Cotswold industry of the future. Woollen cloth, grain, dairy produce, fresh vegetables and by-products of farming, such as tallow, hides and glue, continued to provide a basis for local trade throughout the Roman period, and even towards the end of this, when town markets were in decline, out in the countryside smaller centres continued to serve the local inhabitants and villa owners. Stow was one of these, its role as a market now firmly established.

Without the evidence of inscribed stones or altars, we can only speculate about the religious life of the people at Stow during the Roman occupation. In the Cotswolds, as elsewhere, the newcomers were tolerant towards native forms of worship, always willing to come to terms with the *genius loci*; as a result there were mutual borrowings on both sides with Celts taking up the worship of Roman gods, and having their own recognized and adopted in return. A stone which may have votive significance has been found at Stow; carved into it is a figure of Mars portrayed with a crested helmet, spear and shield. This could be an example of a native god in Roman guise, because although on military sites Mars is essentially the god of war, in Gloucestershire and other civilian areas, while still portrayed as a warrior, he has nothing to do with war but is a fertility god, commonly found in agricultural communities. It would seem that there was little uniformity or rule as to the form of religion in the area, until the official introduction of Christianity in the third century, when the new faith was first taken up by the least Romanized poorer classes outside the towns, as for instance in rural communities like Stow and Lower Slaughter where a collection of sculptures was found in a disused well, as if they had been dumped by fervent Christians anxious to conceal evidence and reminders of their former paganism.

The withdrawal of the Roman armies to defend the mainland territories of their empire at the beginning of the fifth century AD left the Britons at the

Altar stone, a native god in Roman
guise, found at Stow

mercy of the barbarian tribes then threatening the whole of Europe. The
Romanized Celts had lost the habit of fighting and forgotten the arts of war;
and in any case though their smiths had been providing for the military needs
of the Roman army, they had been making only agricultural implements and
domestic tools for native use, so people had no means of defending themselves
properly. Inevitably, therefore, they succumbed to the Angle and Saxon
invaders who approached the Cotswold area from the Midlands and from the
Thames Valley, and in turn established a supremacy over it. The strategic and
economic importance of the region was such that the newcomers continued
to fight for control over it from the sixth until the ninth century, during which
time many of the native Britons were killed and their homes and farmlands
destroyed. The Anglo-Saxons were at first deeply suspicious of any signs of the
Roman occupation and avoided places where these remained, but in time, in
spite of their apprehensions, they infiltrated some country areas including
Stow, where one of their cemeteries has been found. Like the inhabitants they
found there, the newcomers were farmers, so the routine of life and work in
settlements like Stow continued as before, except that the Anglo-Saxon
methods of using land gradually superseded the traditional Celtic ways, fields
being made larger and more regular in size to facilitate the use of larger
ploughs and more hill pasture incorporated with village lands to accommodate

bigger flocks of sheep. The boundaries of Stow were now being extended down the sides of the hill to include some valley land.

The other change brought about by the Anglo-Saxons was the re-introduction of Christianity. Following the withdrawal of the Romans and the severance of connections between Britain and the Roman church in Europe, the practice of Christianity lapsed and the worship of pagan gods was revived in accordance with the beliefs of the invaders. In due course, though, descendants of Christian Romano-Britons, who had fled from the Anglo-Saxons into Wales and thence carried their faith into Ireland, Scotland and Northumbria, began to work their way south through the Midlands to convert Celtic Britons and Anglo-Saxons alike to the Christian faith. They came as missionaries, founding monastic churches as their headquarters whence they travelled out into the countryside preaching, teaching and holding services in the open until they had won enough spiritual and material support to provide for the building of a church. This would be a simple, sturdy building made of local stone by local craftsmen, and once erected would rapidly become the focal point of village life. Conversion to Christianity turned the Anglo-Saxons into fervent and active supporters of the church. Kings granted royal land for building purposes and exempted it from taxation; nobles, too, gave land and money for the upkeep of the monasteries and for the erection of churches on their own estates; thus it was that the first church building at Stow came into existence.

A grant of land for building purposes in the Stow area was first made to the abbey of Evesham in AD 708 by Cynred, King of Mercia, but the earliest reference to an actual building does not occur until 986 AD when Earl Æthelmar, Duke of Cornwall, is said to have erected a church there. At what point the church was given its dedication is uncertain. Currently its patron saint is taken to be Edward the Confessor who died in 1066 and was canonized about a hundred years later. But, according to the Domesday Survey of 1086, the church was already under the protection of an Edward who might have been one of two possibilities: either a legendary saint, a hermit believed to have had a dwelling near the spring on Stow Hill, now known as St Edward's Well; or else Edward the martyr, a kinsman of Earl Æthelmar who built the church in AD 986. The saintliness with which this Edward was endowed by the Anglo-Saxons within a year of his death in AD 978 is a strong argument for the original dedication of the church having been made to him.

The coming of the Normans in 1066 brought to an end what might be termed 'the period of invasions' in the history of Stow. Like previous incursions, the presence of the newcomers inevitably made a difference in the countryside, but more by giving an impetus to developments already taking place than by causing a sharp break with the past. The Normans, primarily

St Edward's Well, a spring with healing powers

warlike by nature and extremely business-like in their management of government, were not impressed with English arrangements for defence or administrative efficiency, so their sense of order and propriety demanded greater regularity in people's lives and in the fulfilment of their obligations – political, economic and religious. The Domesday Survey, inaugurated by William I at Gloucester in 1085, provided him with a comprehensive inventory of his kingdom which he could use as a basis for tax assessment. It also enables us, within limits, to measure the effects of the imposition of Norman overlordship on the land and the future prospects of the country in the light of this.

CHAPTER TWO

Medieval Prosperity

Much of the land in Gloucestershire changed hands as a result of the Conquest, and some around Stow was included in the reward handed out to the Conqueror's follower, Roger de Lacy, who may have been the founder of the castle of which remains have been found near the church at Upper Slaughter. The remainder of the land in the area, including Stow itself, remained in possession of the abbey of Evesham, where Abbot Æthelwig was one of the few English ecclesiastics left in office after the Conquest, being highly esteemed by William, who made him responsible for the maintenance of law and order throughout the West Midlands. Local administration remained much as it had been under the Anglo-Saxon kings, who, for purposes of government, had divided the whole country into shires subdivided into hundreds, with shire and hundred courts providing a link with the central government while dealing with all business concerning people, property and the keeping of the king's peace within the county. However, one change was made that affected Stow. Within the hundred of Salmonsbury (centred on Bourton-on-the-Water) a 'liberty' was created and given as a special privilege and responsibility to the abbey of Evesham. The designated area comprised Stow, Broadwell, Adlestrop, Bourton and Clapton and the new arrangement involved the setting up of a separate court that would deal with matters concerning these places and their inhabitants so that the latter were automatically removed from the jurisdiction of the Salmonsbury hundred court, and granted exemption from the shire court as well.

During the Middle Ages, as overlords of the area, successive abbots of Evesham determined the fortunes of the town and people of Stow. In return for the powers bestowed on them, they paid an annual fee to the Crown, and it was then left to their discretion how their authority was exercised. In respect of the Evesham estates their duties were two-fold: they were guardians of the spiritual welfare of the monastic community and of all those living and working on the abbey lands; they were also responsible for ensuring that these lands produced enough supplies throughout the year to maintain the whole community at Evesham, the abbey itself and any other churches it

St Edward the Confessor, patron saint
of Stow

administered, and that any potentiality for improvement and expansion therein was exploited.

By the time of the Domesday Survey there was already a church building at Stow and a resident priest attached to it. The site of the priest's house is not known, but it would have been near the church and a comfortable dwelling moreover, for a hide of land – and any profits arising from it – went with the church, and in addition the priest was entitled to tithes, that is one tenth of the crops, of the increase of livestock, and of the garden produce of the villagers. He was appointed by the abbey and answerable to it for the maintenance of the chancel of the church, the regular holding of services and the pastoral care of the villagers, always trying to make them mindful of their religious duties. Although there are no remains of the pre-Conquest church, it was almost certainly on the site of the present building; and there are enough fragments of typical Norman stonework left to establish that it was during the reigns of William I and his successors that the church of St Edward took on a cruciform shape, acquired its external buttresses and its pillared aisles inside.

It was probably not so much the work of the priest as the presence of the church in their midst and its close relationship with the routine of their lives that made the greatest impression on this rural community. The church was the only strong building in a village of improvised dwellings made of clay, timber and thatch. Together with its churchyard, under the protection of God's peace, it provided a safe and convenient place for markets, meetings and junketings; while the dovetailing of its calendar with many of the traditional agricultural festivals emphasized the common identity of the church congregation with the village population – Christmas and Easter, for example, afforded holidays after the autumn and spring ploughing and sowing, while Michaelmas coincided with the end of harvest and the start of another farming year. Other Saints' days and festivals provided further welcome breaks in the inexorable routine of field work, for all the workers were expected to observe them as they did the Sabbath.

Lack of education and knowledge among his flock must have made it difficult for any priest, however conscientious, to impart any understanding of the faith to which they were exhorted to subscribe. The churchyard cross, the sculptures in the church, the paintings on the walls would have conveyed more to them than the Latin of the Mass. Nevertheless, there was some religious feeling among them, for it was the congregation who, in addition to paying tithes, gave money to the church for the upkeep of the nave; left bequests of land and property to pay for altar lights, plate and ornaments; and formed The Guild of Holy Trinity to raise funds for the building and maintaining of a chantry in the north aisle. Two other chantries were also added to the aisle, one dedicated to Our Lady and the other to All Saints. In the case of all three, there were means enough for an extra priest to be employed to say prayers for the souls of the charitable on the anniversaries of their deaths; to provide jewels and statues for the adornment of the chapels; and for alms to be given to the poor (The Guild of Holy Trinity in fact maintained nine needy people throughout the year). Charitable gifts and bequests also financed a hospice for the shelter and care of travellers and pilgrims who might be passing through Stow on their way westward to shrines at Winchcombe, Worcester and Hereford, or south and east to Oxford, Salisbury and Winchester. The hospice had been founded in the tenth century by Earl Æthelmar (who built the original church at Stow) and thereafter was maintained by the abbey of Evesham and public alms; evidence of a pre-Conquest timber structure on the site of the present Royalist Hotel – the oldest remaining domestic building in Stow – supports the view that this was where the hospice stood.

As well as caring for the spiritual state of the people in Stow, the abbey of Evesham was responsible for their material well-being. In order to ensure that their lands were being used to the best possible advantage of both the abbey and themselves, the whole of the Stow area, comprising the settlement round the church and the dwellings and fields on the eastern side of the hill, was

The Porch House, now the Royalist Hotel, reputedly the site of an Anglo-Saxon hospice

organized into the manor of Maugersbury and managed, like any other landed estate, by a bailiff appointed by and responsible to the abbey. Primarily he was obliged to see that supplies of produce and money were despatched regularly to the abbey. This necessitated a planned use of resources, supervision of work and careful keeping of records, and it was to facilitate these measures that the manor court existed. Here it was decided what crops should be grown, when ploughing, sowing, harrowing and harvesting should be done, and animals turned on to the stubble or into the meadow. As all the inhabitants were subject to the overlordship of the abbey, so all were required to attend the meetings of the court, and were aware of, and a party to, what went on there. The nature of the dues expected of them was determined by their means and status in the community. Freeholders would pay money rents; less well-off villeins paid their dues in produce together with a short spell of labour service in the fields; and at the bottom of the social scale were the cottagers, with little or no land, whose only means of fulfilling their obligations was through field work, domestic tasks, carting, quarrying and so on. With the exception of the last class, all the tenants of the abbey were enabled to pay the dues required of them by exploiting their right to use the land round the village, held communally by them and their overlord. The arable fields, meadow land and rough pasture were all shared between the villagers and the abbey; those who owed labour services worked on the abbey

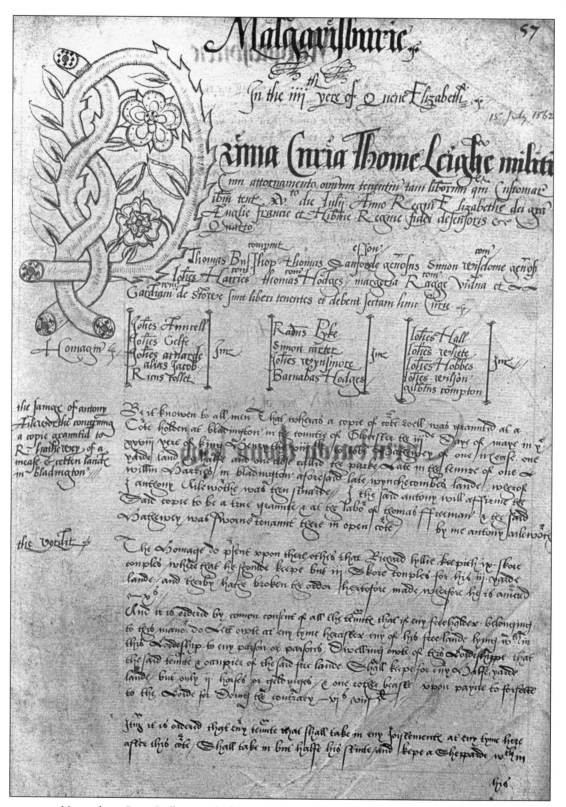

Maugersbury Court Roll, a record of dues and duties owed and paid

land as well as their own; those who owed money rents aimed to produce in excess of their immediate needs so that the surplus could be sold for cash and the rest kept for household use.

However, the economic responsibility of the abbey was not confined merely to making the place pay its way; it also included increasing its profitability if possible. It was clear that, like most rural communities, Stow had an inherent capacity for trade in so far as a whole section of its inhabitants was producing a surplus of farm goods, with the express intention of disposing of the excess by selling it. The community also included people who, as well as labouring in the fields, engaged in weaving and spinning, leatherworking, pottery and tool-making, implementing the results of their farming with money from the sale of their wares. In addition, Stow had particular advantages arising out of its position, which had applied since the first settlers moved into the area: itinerant traders from Wales, the Midlands, the Thames and Severn valleys and the Forest of Dean regularly passed through en route for markets where they could sell or exchange their goods. These transients afforded people in Stow an opportunity to provide food, shelter and stabling, to sell some of their own goods for retailing elsewhere and to acquire raw materials not available locally. The arrival of travellers, at whatever season or on whatever day of the week, was likely to lead to

Market Cross, a medieval shaft with a nineteenth-century gable top

spontaneous marketing. The regular interchange of goods between Stow inhabitants themselves and with dwellers in the neighbourhood tended to take place on a fixed day in the week, usually on Sunday when people were free, thus becoming a regular feature of the weekly round.

The abbots of Evesham, keen to run their estates at a profit, were quick to recognize that the encouragement of a market on estate land might have a definite advantage if, in return for certain concessions to market holders, the overlord could ensure an outlet for surplus products from his estates, a source of necessary and luxury goods for himself at reasonable prices and a steady income from market profits. The Norman kings themselves favoured such a policy by claiming that all trade was under the protection of the Crown and best channelled into centres with privileged status, where it could be controlled, supervised and safeguarded. So when the abbot of Evesham appealed to Henry I in 1107 for official recognition of the market at Stow and basic privileges for it, these were readily granted and set down in the terms of the first charter. This gave the abbot and his tenants the right to have a market on Thursday each week and to make what arrangements they chose to ensure the safety, efficiency and honesty of the proceedings. That the charter was an advantage both to the overlord and the community concerned is proved by requests for it to be confirmed whenever there was any possibility of its being challenged, and by attempts at regular intervals to have more privileges added to it. Thus a confirmation issued in 1126 included a further concession granting the abbot and the community the right to pay any dues in respect of the market directly into the Exchequer, thus leaving the organizing of financial affairs entirely in the hands of the townsfolk and safeguarding the latter from interference by any royal officials. Two other charters secured to Stow the right to hold fairs in addition to weekly markets. The first, granted by Edward III in 1330, established a yearly fair to be held in August; the second, granted by Edward IV in 1476, allowed two fairs to be held – 'one fair on the feast of Saints Philip and James to begin two days immediately preceding that feast and to last two days immediately following, and a second fair to be kept on the feast of the Translation of St Edward King and Confessor'. (Incidentally, here is a clear indication that by this time Edward the Martyr has been replaced by Edward the Confessor as patron saint of the church.)

The most significant result of Stow's official recognition as a market centre and self-governing community was its transformation from a village into an urban settlement, where, among a population once largely agricultural, there now appeared some townsmen with commercial interests. The market established by charter had to be regulated in so far as only on the appointed day in the week would the place be geared to outdoor buying and selling

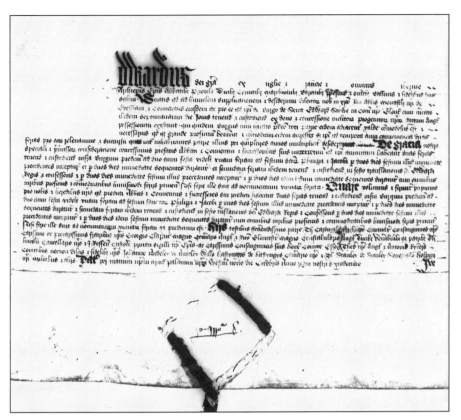

The Charter of 1476 granted by Edward IV

with all the arrangements for these in operation. The churchyard, where the market had begun, no longer seemed convenient enough for a properly organized occasion, so a more extensive site was found in the present Square which was accessible from several directions, and where there was ample room for booths, animal pens, carts, oxen and horses. Moreover, all business was brought under the supervision of market officials whose responsibility it was to ensure that nothing happened to disturb the peace of the occasion and the good name of the place.

The siting of the market in the Square now made this the focal point of the settlement; those who could afford to, and wanted to benefit from the market, established new dwellings in the vicinity, properly built houses with doors and windows at the front opening on to the Square, and long rectangular garden plots stretching out behind – typical medieval town holdings, the basic pattern of which is still visible from the air today. The acquisition of land and a house adjacent to the Square necessitated new tenancy agreements whereby in return for paying a money rent (as opposed to payments in kind or labour service) the holders gained privileges in respect of the market: exemption from tolls, for example, on goods bought and sold on market days; personal status as residents of Stow; freedom of choice as regards their occupations, and of movement to come and go as they pleased, unlike tenants tied to their property by labour services.

The introduction of more regulations than had previously applied on market days called for officials to enforce them and a new court to deal exclusively with matters of trade and the interests of those engaged in it. So, an area now defined as 'the township of Stow' was carved out of the manor of Maugersbury, its residents being served by the new court, while the tenants of Maugersbury continued to be answerable to the manor court that dealt with their agricultural activities. In due course the existence of the two courts was to lead to a great deal of controversy between the people of Stow and those of Maugersbury, but while both areas and their courts remained under the jurisdiction of the abbots of Evesham, the arrangement worked quite smoothly.

Official recognition of the market at Stow did not radically affect the nature of the trade that had been going on there for so long. As always, the main object of the occasion was to enable the townsfolk to procure foodstuffs and other essential supplies for themselves, and to afford rural customers an opportunity to buy goods made in the town – bread and ale, cloth and clothes, leather and metal goods, tools, baskets, ropes, etc.; while craftsmen needed the market to provide them with raw materials for their work – wood, iron, flax, dyes, wool, etc. The timing of markets was carefully arranged so that places within easy distance of each other had their markets on different days. Thus people from Moreton or Northleach could do business at Stow without missing market day in their own towns; and Stow traders could go farther afield to sell their goods. Once a market was seen to be thriving, it attracted traders from an ever-widening radius, and though basically a local institution, it was never narrowly parochial.

Busy and prosperous as the Stow market undoubtedly was, it could not compare with the fairs which came to have both national and international importance. Because they happened less often and were on so much larger a scale than the markets, they were more formally and more strictly regulated. They were opened and closed at a set time by a proclamation; injunctions regarding the conduct of business were announced publicly; and for the duration, special officers attached to a particular court were appointed to deal with any breaches of the regulations, or legal business arising out of fair activities. Not only did the fairs exceed the markets in size, they brought a

Chadwell Tombs at Broadwell, belonging to a wool-trading family

new dimension into the trade of the town because of the many strangers and foreigners who attended them, bringing unusual and exotic goods for sale. There were, first of all, the English traders who came into the Cotswold area from the Midlands, South Wales, the Severn and Thames valleys, with foodstuffs, livestock and raw materials in greater variety than would have been seen at local markets. Then, secondly, there were the traders who came from the ports, in particular London, Bristol and Southampton, most of them foreigners, because the bulk of trade between England and the continent was carried out by foreign merchants, who were not as reluctant as the English to travel far afield. It was the people with foreign goods to sell who introduced a colourful and exciting element to the fair, for their wares included wines, exotic fruits and spices; dyes and other essentials for cloth and leather workers; and luxuries such as carpets and fine materials. The Italian and Flemish merchants came primarily to buy wool, but they would visit whatever fairs they could while in the area, and were welcomed not only for the goods they carried but also because – forbidden to take gold and silver out of the country – they were obliged to spend their profits here.

The fair was designed as a major occasion for buying and selling; housewives, stewards from wealthy households, and representatives of abbots aimed to buy in bulk here and stock up with necessities and rarities for the

The distinctive tower of Stow church, a symbol of medieval prosperity

months ahead. For Stow people, just as important as the buying and selling was the fact that visitors might need help with loading and unloading goods, accommodation, food, stabling, the services of a blacksmith, a wheelwright or a saddler – all of which meant increased business for craftsmen and casual labourers. Accommodation was temporarily made available to travellers; there were larger supplies of bread and cooked meats on sale; and (according to tradition) every house on the Square was turned into an alehouse or at any rate sold drink during the fairs. The church benefited too. Townsfolk and visitors alike attended special services for the feast day associated with the fair; traders offered prayers for success in business, and travellers for their safety on the roads; and all who could afford, donated money to the church.

The regularity of the fairs made them red-letter days in the calendar to such an extent that many other events were dated by them. Stow fair became established as the time when contracts were drawn up and completed, leases entered upon and workers hired. Even places outside Stow used the date of its fair to fix limits in property leases and manorial records; and up to fairly recent times, human ages and activities were reckoned according to the date of the fair: 'He was 70 last Stow fair'; 'She'll be dead two years come next Stow fair'; and even 'It's as certain as the fair.' In another way too, the occasion of the fair was significant, since it was a holiday for all who attended, whether they came to do serious business or merely to mingle with the crowd, enjoying unaccustomed sights and sounds, avoiding or yielding to temptation in the abundance of food, ribbons and laces, charms and jewellery: and on the Saints' days associated with the fairs, joining in the religious processions that wound round the church and out into the Square accompanied by dancing, singing and playing.

As has been said, most of the foreign merchants came to the Cotswolds primarily to buy the products of 'the sheep with long faces, square bodies and the whitest wool' (Leland), which were kept in huge flocks throughout the area. The wool was needed to support the cloth industry in the Low Countries and northern Italy, and was so vital that, to make certain of an uninterrupted supply, merchants often bought it sight unseen and a year in advance. This risk was not as great as it might seem because Cotswold wool had the reputation of being the best available in England (except for that from the Leominster area); it might cost three times as much as any other, but it rarely disappointed. The large number of flocks in the Cotswolds, belonging to monastic and lay owners, ensured that both English merchants of the staple and foreign traders had ample sources of supply to satisfy their needs. The wool trade was so vast, so profitable and so stable that many of those engaged in it became extremely wealthy and well known, for having made a success of their business, they had to let others know of their success by ostentatious spending on themselves, on their parish church and on charitable causes. Few of Stow's benefactors are known by name, but the rebuilding of the chancel of the church and the addition of the south aisle in the fourteenth century, and the building of the present distinctive tower in the fifteenth century showed that the town was prospering along with the rest of the area. The almshouses, also erected in the fifteenth century, were the gift of William Chester, a merchant stapler, whose father Richard had already presented Stow with its market cross.

Gradually the trade in Cotswold wool came to be concentrated in certain places, the fairs of which were given over almost exclusively to this business. Stow fair never became a specialized one like these, perhaps because for so long trade in the town had successfully included a variety of goods; but it did become famed for the large number of sheep bought and sold there, and Sheep Street is said to have acquired its name because it was used to accommodate the overflow of animals from the Square. Situated in the midst of an area where sheep keeping was an integral part of local husbandry, Stow was a natural centre for the marketing of sheep, but equally important were hides, leather and leather goods, cloth, cheeses and meat; and this is one reason why – when other fairs lost their importance as the trade in wool declined – the fairs at Stow continued to prosper.

CHAPTER THREE

Peace and War in the Sixteenth and Seventeenth Centuries

During the course of the sixteenth century a radical change took place in the character and outlook of the people in Stow, which was to shift the focal point of life in the town from the church to the market place. This was due partly to the policy of the Tudor monarchs, rulers throughout the century, and partly to contemporary economic circumstances in England and in Europe. The rule of the Tudors, which brought peace and prosperity to the country as a whole, naturally benefited Stow, just as their centralized administration made the town aware of the power of the government to interfere in local affairs. Of the sovereigns themselves, the people of Stow could only have had indirect knowledge. Both Henry VII and Henry VIII made their way through the county to Gloucester without visiting the Cotswold area; but Sudeley Castle was the scene of lavish spectacle when Queen Elizabeth stayed there during her progresses and people from Stow may have journeyed to Winchcombe to celebrate her coming and thereafter boast of having seen her in person.

More directly, Stow felt the effects of Henry VIII's reformation of the church in England. The dissolution of the monasteries (1536–9) ended the hold of Evesham Abbey over the township and the neighbouring manor of Maugersbury; rights in both of these passed through several hands until they came into possession of the Chamberlayne family – Maugersbury in 1598 and Stow in 1603. So by the end of the century the whole area was under lay administration and dues formerly paid to Evesham went to the new overlord. The latter also became responsible for the appointment of the rectors of the church, who in turn were answerable to the bishopric of Gloucester, a new diocese established out of the proceeds of the sale of monastic property in the county. Every church service was now in English, as laid down in the English Book of Common Prayer (issued in 1549), and people heard a sermon in the course of it. As this needed to be listened to in a quiet and orderly fashion, pews and a pulpit were introduced into the body of the church, where formerly the congregation had stood as silent spectators, while the priest celebrated Mass at the altar. The removal of statues, lights and ornaments from the three chapels in the north aisle, the whitewashing of interior walls and the banning of processions round the town on Saints' days, robbed the church and its ceremonies of much of their former colour and life, but the congregation necessarily went along with what the royal governors of the church required of them.

Changing economic circumstances proved of great benefit to Stow. The discovery of the New World and expansion of trade there steadily enhanced the importance of Bristol and Gloucester as ports, and not only they, but also the whole of their hinterland, in other words the Cotswold area, shared in the new raw materials and products coming from abroad and the new markets opened up there for goods exported from England. Keeping pace with the increased trade in the ports, there was a marked expansion of inland trade so that a place like Stow, with weekly markets and two fairs in the year, had an opportunity to handle more business in connection with both local goods and those passing to and from the ports. Heavier traffic through the town called for more accommodation and facilities for the conduct of business, so any people and places (it was usually the inns) capable of providing these were likely to profit. As carrier services expanded to meet the demand for transport, so more horses were needed, and by the end of the century these were beginning to feature prominently at the fairs. Finally, the century saw a very marked growth in the size and population of London, which stimulated the demand there for food and consumer goods that necessarily had to be obtained from an ever-widening hinterland. This stretched as far as Gloucestershire, whence the capital drew much of its cheese, bacon, meat and barley, Lechlade at the head of navigation on the Thames being a convenient transit point for goods from the Cotswold area to be sent.

There is no way of making an accurate assessment of the size of the population of Stow during the sixteenth century, but it is likely that numbers were increasing with economic progress, and that though small by today's standards (probably about 800) Stow would have qualified for Leland's description of similar places as 'a great market town replenished with much people'. By the end of the century the community was predominantly one of tradesmen and craftsmen, some following pursuits linked with country needs, for example smiths, wheelwrights and ropemakers; and some essentially urban occupations made worthwhile by the existence of a non-agricultural element in the town and by the extra business created by the markets and fairs, for example bakers, clothworkers and candlemakers.

In addition to the natives, there had now appeared the first of what might be called an alien élite: people from London who had made money in the capital and thus been enabled to buy estates in the country and settle there. These included William Chester and Richard Shepham, charitable

The Court House and lock-up, symbols of civic authority

benefactors of the town, Sir Thomas Leigh, once Lord Mayor of London, who came into possession of Maugersbury at the time of the Reformation and then parted with it to the Chamberlaynes (a family that had been in government service), while he acquired lands for his own family at Longborough, Adlestrop and Broadwell. A few years later, in the early seventeenth century, Lower Swell was taken over by another Londoner, Sir William Courteen, who in due course sold his estate to Sir Robert Atkyns, Baron of the Exchequer, whose son Robert, the noted historian of Gloucestershire, later succeeded to the estate. Meanwhile at the other end of the social scale, local poor – hitherto relieved in their distress by the church and charitable bequests – were being augmented by vagrants, victims of hardship elsewhere, who frequented the many roads that passed through Stow. Usually resentful of interference on the part of the central government, the townsfolk were nevertheless thankful to adopt and put into practice the successive Poor Laws passed during the century to deal with what was becoming a national problem, for these limited the responsibility of the community to those who belonged to it, and allowed any without a legitimate call on its charity to be turned away.

The town itself was now growing in size and assuming a shape still recognizable today. The original timber dwellings facing the Square were being replaced by typical town houses built of stone in the 'Cotswold' style, with steeply pitched roofs, high gables and moulded dripstones over the windows and front doors. Local stone quarries and limepits, and the presence of masons, slaters and carpenters in the town were sources of material and labour. The need of an increasing population for more homes was met by infilling, the building of dwellings in the garden strips behind the Square, access to these being afforded by narrow tures or alleys which can still be seen. As well as having the best private dwellings round it, the Square also acquired some public buildings and landmarks which underlined the increasing urban consciousness of the townsfolk. There was, for example, the Court House in the south-west corner – meeting place of the town court and the manorial court of Maugersbury, and adjoining it a cellar that served as a lock-up. Nearby was the Grammar School, 'for the instruction of boys and children in the Latin tongue and other more polite literature and science'; this was founded in 1594 by Richard Shepham, who also rebuilt and re-endowed the almshouses which stood in the churchyard and afforded homes for nine poor people. On the south side of the Square was the market cross erected in the fifteenth century and consisting of a monolithic shaft set on two steps and an octagonal base, the shaft possibly being of great age. (The gabled headstone

The Grammar School founded in 1594; now the Masonic Hall

was added when the cross was restored in the nineteenth century, but recalls the early history of the town, since the carving in two of the niches at the top depicts the abbot of Evesham receiving the town charter, and Richard Shepham cradling the church tower in his arm.) Facing this was the Cross House, a storage place for the hurdles and other equipment used at the markets and fairs. In the north-east corner of the Square stood the stocks, the instrument of summary justice meted out by the town court to eavesdroppers, scolds and petty criminals.

Though as yet there were no permanent buildings in the open centre of the Square, this part of Stow was the most congested, for during the Middle Ages the main line of the Fosse Way had been diverted (for the advantage of the markets and fairs) into the Square, along its west side and out again along

Maugersbury Manor and grounds, home of the Chamberlayne family

Ragg's Row, a seventeenth-century extension of the town

present Church Street to rejoin its original course. The road from Chipping Norton also came into the Square via Digbeth Street and left via Church Street. The present Sheep Street, as has been mentioned elsewhere, was no more than an overflow area for the market. Round the Square and along the approaches to it were the inns and alehouses, but the buildings have changed their uses so often since the sixteenth century that it is impossible to attach names with certainty to them, though we know there were among them the Apothecaries', Mercers' and Grocers' arms, the Swan, the Bell, the Crown and the George. Beyond the immediate vicinity of the Square, development was beginning along Ragg's Row and Well Lane and down the road towards Maugersbury; but Maugersbury itself remained essentially rural except for the new manor house built for the Chamberlaynes, and the park planned as a setting for it at the end of the sixteenth century. Here there were still open spaces and gardens around the houses, straying animals and occasional trees, reminders of the agricultural nature of the original settlement.

On the whole the sixteenth century had brought peace and prosperity to the townsfolk of Stow, and they had every reason to expect continuing progress in the years ahead. However, the accession of the Stuarts in 1603 and changes in governmental policy ushered in a period of tension that was to end in the outbreak of Civil War in 1642 and a complete disruption of normal life. Though Gloucestershire was some distance away from London, the centre of political events, it was not immune from the repercussions of Stuart policy that affected the country as a whole; moreover, because of the close trade connections between London and Gloucestershire, the people in this area were well supplied with news and ahead of many other provincial communities in their outlook and ideas; consequently all the basic causes of war can be discerned in their attitudes in the early seventeenth century.

Already social jealousies were beginning to cause a rift in county society, giving rise to a distrust and dislike of aristocratic authority, especially when exercised by men whose fortunes had been improved by royal favour. During the early years of the century the townsfolk of Stow engaged in expensive litigation with their overlord Edmund Chamberlayne in order to defend their status as a self-governing community. Ultimately the authority of Chamberlayne prevailed, but jealousy and resentment over the control of the markets and fairs (and of course of their profits) continued to rankle. Again, in so far as it was the gentry who were responsible for administrative duties in the county, they were identified in people's minds with repressive royal policies; thus Lord Chandos of Sudeley, Lord Lieutenant of the county in charge of mustering the array, together with William Leigh of Adlestrop, High Sheriff, saddled with the duty of collecting Ship Money (one of the special taxes imposed by Charles I in the 1630s) were both resented by the local populace who 'much abhorred to be betrayed to slavery *by one of their own county*'.

Another grievance arose from a slump in the cloth trade, chiefly as a result of the Thirty Years War in Europe (1618–48), though Gloucestershire clothiers and associated workers blamed it on royal favour shown to London cloth merchants. Stow's fortunes were affected in so far as trade at markets and fairs was reduced; dyers, weavers and woolcombers in the community were left idle; and other traders, for example builders, masons, leather-workers, etc., suffered proportionately as ready money was in shorter supply and there were fewer demands for their services. Equally deeply, the people felt uneasy about the religious policy of the Stuarts, in particular of Charles I and his Archbishop of Canterbury William Laud, formerly Dean of Gloucester, known and disliked in the county for his interfering ways. Admittedly, the majority of people since the Reformation had been less awed and dominated by religious authorities than previously, but they still took a pride in their parish church and subscribed to its maintenance, and they did not want any direction from above as to how it should be managed and its services conducted. Townsfolk in Stow were following trends elsewhere in favouring a Puritanical form of Protestantism rather than Laud's ritualistic

St Edward's church, with sixteenth-century almshouses in the background

one, perhaps because this tied in with their growing sense of urban independence and responsibility for managing their own affairs. Thus, when war was declared in 1642, many people in Gloucestershire had already decided where their loyalties lay. Given a choice, members of all classes would have preferred to remain aloof from the conflict altogether; but in persons of consequence it was considered an evasion of responsibility not to take sides, and ordinary folk – in self-defence – were often forced into association with one party or the other. Once the war started, people in Gloucestershire, and in Stow particularly, found themselves in an area of vital significance, which made it impossible for them to remain either disaffected or unaffected. Economically the county was rich in agricultural and industrial resources and had ports along the Severn with useful trade connections and rich merchant populations. Strategically it straddled the main land routes between Wales, the

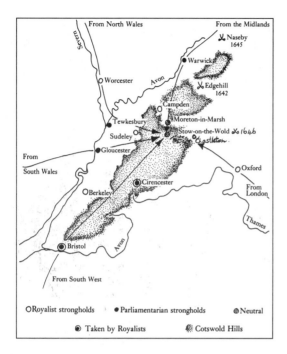

From North Wales
From the Midlands
Naseby 1645
Warwick
Worcester
Avon
Edgehill 1642
Campden
Tewkesbury
Moreton-in-Marsh
Sudeley
Stow-on-the-Wold 1646
Chastleton
Gloucester
From South Wales
Oxford
From London
Berkeley
Cirencester
Thames
Bristol
Avon
From South West

○ Royalist strongholds   ● Parliamentarian strongholds   ◉ Neutral
◉ Taken by Royalists   ▦ Cotswold Hills

Map showing the strategic significance of Stow during the Civil Wars

Midlands, the Thames Valley and the South-West, and contained some of the river routes and crossings connected with the Thames, the Severn and their tributaries; in addition it had an abundance of country houses capable of being garrisoned by small forces that could be used for harassing enemies in the surrounding countryside; and four highly desirable key points: Bristol, Gloucester, Cirencester and Tewkesbury.

During the first Civil War, Stow saw a very considerable amount of activity because of its position in relation to the routes across the north Cotswolds, which were constantly being used by troops of both sides passing between their own strongholds or on their way to attack those of the enemy. Though without defences or armed defenders (in 1608, only seventy-four men in the town were listed as capable of bearing arms), its hilltop commanded a good view of the surrounding countryside, its numerous inns and town houses afforded food and shelter for men and horses, and its farriers, blacksmiths, wheelwrights, leatherworkers and toolmakers were available to supply their services when needed. Nearby were several estates owned by prosperous families – the Leighs at Adlestrop, the Jones's at Chastleton, the Chamberlaynes at Maugersbury, the Whitmores at Slaughter – whose menfolk were equipped with arms and horses, and where the fields and barns held valuable reserves of livestock, carts, saddlery, fodder and cereals. For the

The King's Arms sheltered Charles I during his wartime visits to Stow

first two years of the war the townsfolk also tried to keep up their markets and fairs so that local farmers and traders from further afield made their way to the town at regular intervals, a boon to the marauding soldiery of both sides on the lookout for an easy way to implement their supplies.

Once the king established his headquarters at Oxford in 1642, it became an essential factor in Royalist strategy to secure control of the south-west Midlands and the whole of Gloucestershire; Worcester and Tewkesbury, the castles of Berkeley and Sudeley, and nearly all the country houses were already in loyal hands, but Charles also wanted to be sure of Bristol, Gloucester and Cirencester in order to secure the lines of communication with the South-West and Wales, his chief recruiting grounds. Parliament, with its headquarters in London and known sympathizers in the aforementioned towns, hoped to strengthen its hold on them in order to hamper the movements of Royalist troops and the king's attempts to use the Gloucestershire area as a source of recruits and supplies.

The first appearance of troops in Stow was in December 1642, when the Marquess of Hertford with regiments from Wales stayed in the town for five days en route for Oxford, where he hoped to impress on the king the importance of Cirencester to the Royalist war effort in the county. The quartering of twenty officers and horses and 120 foot soldiers cost John Chamberlayne £5 a day, and presumably other Stow dwellers were put to similar expense. On the strength of Hertford's advice, the king sent Prince Rupert with regiments of horse to take Cirencester. These also passed through Stow where food and shelter for men and horses were provided. The taking of Cirencester in February 1643 should have left the Royalists in peaceful possession of the Cotswold area, but instead it roused the Parliamentary garrison in Gloucester into taking the offensive, and presently Stow was subjected to a raid by troops from the city, who came to confront any Royalists they could find.

The town next saw action later in 1643 at the time of the siege of Gloucester. The king, following the capture of Cirencester and Bristol, had marched on the city and surrounded it, with the idea of starving out the inhabitants. Meanwhile the Parliamentarians in London, advised of the worsening situation in Gloucester, hastily raised a force of new recruits and London-trained bands and despatched it under the leadership of the Earl of Essex to raise the siege. Essex and his men advanced from London via Aylesbury, Bicester and Chipping Norton. The weather was bad and they made slower progress than expected in spite of forced marches and only hasty stops en route. The last of these, before they reached Gloucester, was made between Adlestrop and Stow where the men camped out in the fields, taking advantage of any shelter afforded by hedges and trees. They were not without food, however, since John Chamberlayne was forced to give them 'household provisions of bread, beere, cheese, meate and provender' to the cost of £6. When news of the approaching relief force reached the king at Gloucester, he decided to send Prince Rupert with a troop of horse to intercept it. Rupert caught up with Essex at Stow, but could do no more with his horsemen than ride round and harry the flanks of the Parliamentary foot soldiers who were resuming their march on Gloucester, shoulder to shoulder in compact ranks. Eventually Rupert began to retreat ahead of them and returned to Gloucester, his mission abortive. The people of Stow heard of the subsequent raising of the siege by Essex and his men, when the king and part of his army withdrawing from Gloucester went through the town en route for Newbury, where they overtook and attacked some of the Parliamentarians on their way back to London after the siege.

From this point onwards until 1646 there was no more fighting in the vicinity of Stow, but troops belonging to both sides frequently passed through the town and sometimes quartered there for several days at a time. Always free board and lodging were demanded of the townsfolk, and most of the time stealing went on as well, neither side being better than the other so far as discipline was concerned. Meanwhile, at regular intervals, contributions had to be paid to the Parliamentary garrison at Gloucester and to the Royalist garrisons at Worcester, Winchcombe and Chipping Campden. Like many others, Stow people had no option about complying with demands made of them. Acquiescence gained at least a temporary immunity; and what they failed to give willingly would have been taken from them anyway. The importance of Stow as a strategic point can be gauged by the number of eminent leaders from the armies who were there from time to time: Fairfax, Waller, Massey and Essex with Parliamentarian troops; Wilmot, Hertford and Prince Rupert with Royalists. The king himself was at Stow twice more

Sudeley Castle, a Royalist stronghold

during the course of the war: in June 1644, and again in May 1645 when he was accompanied by a thousand horse and foot soldiers and is said to have spent a night at the King's Arms, 'the best inn between London and Worcester'.

When the final battle of the war came to be fought at Stow in 1646, the situation both in Gloucestershire and in the country as a whole had changed radically. Though the king was still holding out at his headquarters in Oxford, the tide of events was turning against him and most of his followers were now thoroughly disheartened. One exception was Sir Jacob Astley, the governor of Worcester, who was still in command of a strong body of troops. In March 1646 the king ordered him to proceed with his forces from Worcester to Oxford, promising that he would be met by a convoy on the way. However, messages went astray and fell into the hands of the enemy, so that by the time Astley got on the move, Parliamentary troops had begun to close in on him from all directions. Finally he was completely surrounded on the hillside to the north of Stow, and there at dawn on 21 March the two armies came face to face. The Parliamentarians had the advantage of superior numbers and were confident of success, but the Royalists fought 'with the despair of veterans who had not a battle more to win or lose'. Twice they nearly broke through the ring of enemies surrounding them, but at last they began to retreat into Stow, where fighting continued right into the centre of the town and, according to local legend, blood flowed down the steep slope of Digbeth Street and the narrow tures leading out of the Square.

Then with two hundred of his men killed and the remainder taken prisoner, Astley himself surrendered, his captors, out of respect for his grey hairs and outstanding courage, bringing him a regimental drum to sit on, whence he uttered his prophetic statement: 'You may now sit and play for you have done all your work, if you fall not out among yourselves'. As it was the strongest building in the town the church was used to house the prisoners overnight and about 1,600 in all were crowded together there, little consideration being given to their needs or comfort. In due course traces of the battle were removed, but one lasting memorial remains in the church where an incised stone slab covers the grave of Captain Hastings Keyt, a Royalist officer slain in the battle and here depicted in full uniform with his lace-edged sash, helmet, gauntlets, pike and musket. Astley's failure to reach Oxford with reinforcements was the final blow to the Royalist hopes. Soon after the battle of Stow, the king surrendered and thus brought the first Civil War to a close.

Five years later Stow was caught up in national events once more when Charles I's eldest son, having inherited the Stuart cause after the execution of his father, made a gallant bid to regain the crown. Having been defeated at

Sir Jacob Astley, leader of the Royalists defeated at Stow

the battle of Worcester in 1651, he tried to make his way south in an attempt to escape to France, riding towards Bristol and passing through Chipping Campden, Stow and Cirencester en route. Close in pursuit of him and those who had fought with him at Worcester came troopers of the New Model Army. They failed to capture the prince, but did catch up with Royalist Arthur Jones who had fled home to Chastleton to hide himself; he then had to escape by night while his pursuers slept heavily, having supped well and

Memorial in Stow church to Hastings Keyt, killed in the battle at Stow

drunk considerably more than was good for them of drugged wine supplied by Mistress Jones.

From the end of the wars until the restoration of Charles II in 1660, the whole country came under the control of the New Model Army and was made to realize the difference between monarchical and military-backed republican rule. For people in Stow, as elsewhere, heavy taxation, the dislocation of trade and business and work on the land, created a difficult situation with little hope of improvement because losses incurred during the war by townsfolk and farmers alike, through authorized requisitioning and unlicensed stealing, left them without means of subsistence and livelihood, while the passage of horses and heavy wagons and frequent skirmishing had played havoc with the roads and left the countryside scarcely recognizable. Further limitations on life and enterprise were the moral restrictions imposed by strict Puritanical practices in respect of religion, reflected in the replacement of the town's popular rector Roland Wilde by one readier to comply with governmental requirements.

Small wonder then that the simultaneous restoration of the old constitution and Established Church in 1660 was welcomed in Stow with much bell-ringing and public rejoicing, and that people felt they could now look and

Chastleton House whence Arthur Jones escaped after the Battle of Worcester, 1651

plan ahead with greater confidence and optimism. But recovery came slowly, and evidently money remained in short supply, since twenty years later the bishop of Gloucester sent a gift to the churchwardens of Stow 'because the parish church hath become very ruinous and not able to have been repaired by the inhabitants of the said parish unlesse assisted by others' charity'. The obtrusion of national politics into the affairs of the town had certainly undermined its fortunes for the time being, but survival indicated an underlying resilience that has always been a factor in Stow's continuing existence.

CHAPTER FOUR

Eighteenth-Century Renaissance

For Stow, the eighteenth century resembled the sixteenth century in so far as a stable political background created a favourable setting for economic and social advance. The period of peace that followed the accession in 1714 of George I, first of the Hanoverian dynasty, afforded those concerned with agriculture, industry and trade an opportunity to engage in and profit from their activities without interruption; it was therefore a period of affluence, in

A portrait by Thomas Beach of James Leigh and his family, patrons of Stow traders and craftsmen

Adlestrop House, home of the Leigh family

which many people used their wealth to make their own lives more comfortable and pleasurable, and to encourage experiment and investment in new ventures, thus spreading the effects of their prosperity more widely.

Because agriculture still played a major part in its economy, Gloucestershire was inevitably much affected by the changes taking place generally in farming during the century. Much of the land round Stow, owned by the Leigh and Chamberlayne families, had already undergone improvement during the previous century. By agreements between tenants and landlords, some farmers, instead of communal holdings in the village fields, now had small fields which were theirs to enclose and work separately just as they wished. In Maugersbury and Adlestrop innovations such as a rotation of food crops, the introduction of new fodder crops and a combination of stock rearing and arable farming, were already being tried out – ahead of many other farming regions in England. And though in some areas the enclosing of land by estate owners and yeoman farmers led to hardship and discontent, this did not happen round Stow, where most smallholders got the land they wanted in return for their share in the village fields; no one was forced to give up their farm and become a dependent labourer; and enough coverts and coppices were left for the cutting of wood for fuel and repairs, and for sporting purposes. It was as a result of the final enclosure at Maugersbury that the rector of Stow was awarded an allotment of land in lieu of tithe, and used some of this to plant the beech woodland beside the Fosse Way up the hill to Stow, a notable feature of the local landscape until destroyed by recent storms.

In the southern part of Gloucestershire the eighteenth century saw the beginning of industrial as well as agricultural change. The north Cotswolds had few of the necessary conditions for large-scale industry, but there were enough people in market towns like Stow with traditional skills to enable them to satisfy the growing needs of an urban and rural population both locally and elsewhere. In the past, the trades and crafts practised had largely been those of the countryside based on the products of the land, but now these had to be adjusted to more sophisticated demands. Stow had always had its leatherworkers who either tanned their own hides or, in the eighteenth century, bought from a local tannery situated behind the present Park Street. Expanding trade at markets and fairs in skins and hides produced a steady supply of leather, while increasing work on the farms and in the carrying trade ensured a corresponding demand for saddlery, straps, harness and material for the building and repair of coaches now appearing on the roads in steadily growing numbers. In addition there was a demand for boots, shoes and gloves, since as well as the townsfolk, people from the surrounding countryside depended on Stow tradesmen for supplying and repairing their footwear. An apprentice shoemaker, who learned his trade in Stow and then went up to London to work, made a pair of such well-fitting shoes for George III's wife Caroline, that she promptly ordered forty more pairs.

Spinning, weaving and dyeing were also traditional occupations in Stow. Originally these were practised to meet local demands, but as production in the cloth trade further south in Gloucestershire was stepped up, Stow workers benefited from the clothiers' policy of sending out wool to spinners and weavers working in their own homes. In addition there was a call for similar work nearer at hand, since at this time silk mills were operating at Stow, Donnington and Blockley and a linen factory at Moreton-in-Marsh, providing employment both for those prepared to go so far to work and those who undertook tasks in their own houses – often women and children. Cheeses continued to be an important feature of Stow markets and fairs; the making and storing of these created a need for cheese cloth and sieves. The factory at Moreton produced cloth and sieves were made at Stow, the wooden frames being the work of the craftsmen who also made wheels, carts, field gates, hurdles and farm implements.

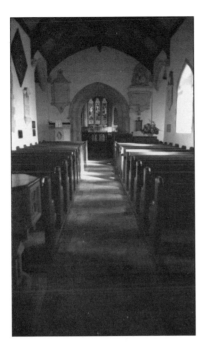

The interior of Adlestrop church, the work of Stow carpenters and masons

Woodworkers found further employment in connection with the building trade, which also prospered during the century when farms were being enlarged and improved, and private dwellings rebuilt or given elaborate additions to satisfy their owners' desires to keep up with the contemporary fashions. Craftsmen were needed to supply doors, window frames and panelling and were commissioned to make special pieces of furniture; Stow carpenters were employed when the interior of Adlestrop church was renovated. Building occupied quarrymen, masons, slaters and plasterers as well, and again these worked not just in Stow itself but in the surrounding countryside. In the town Stow Lodge and the Unicorn Hotel are basically eighteenth-century buildings; also St Edward's House in the Square, with its elaborate façade of fluted Corinthian pilasters. Nearby, James Leigh's house, Adlestrop Park, refurbished in the 1770s, and Warren Hastings' house at Daylesford, rebuilt in the 1790s, were both products of local labour working in local material to realize the designs of fashionable architects. Other thriving industries, important to both town and country dwellers, involved smiths and braziers working in iron and brass to supply domestic and farming equipment; makers of candles and soap; and weavers of twigs and straw who supplied the town haberdashers and milliners with baskets, cradles and straw bonnets to sell.

Lime kiln in Camp Gardens, important to
Stow builders

Perhaps the main factor boosting Stow's prosperity during the eighteenth
century was the improvement in the roads, which for centuries had shaped the
economic life and social pattern of the area. Although since Elizabeth's reign
the roads had been the responsibility of the Justices of the Peace, who were
empowered to conscript labour and requisition material for their upkeep, the
task was largely a fruitless one and, except in the immediate vicinity of towns,
road surfaces continued hazardous, with deep ruts filled with mud in winter
and dust in summer. The introduction of Turnpike Trusts, therefore, marked a
big step forward. This was an arrangement whereby a small group of people
bought an interest in a stretch of road and then took responsibility for its
upkeep, repaying themselves for their initial and subsequent outlay by charging
tolls for the use of it. At first there was a furious outcry against the turnpikes
and people avoided using them, but in time the benefits of more comfortable
journeys for travellers and safer transport for goods were acknowledged,
accepted and paid for without demur. Stow, at the hub of a number of
established routes, gained considerably from the turnpiked roads in the area,
also being linked to the main routes to London through Chipping Norton and
Burford. There was an enormous increase in the amount of traffic in and out
of the town, goods and passenger services were expanded, and the need for
inns and posting services became greater than ever.

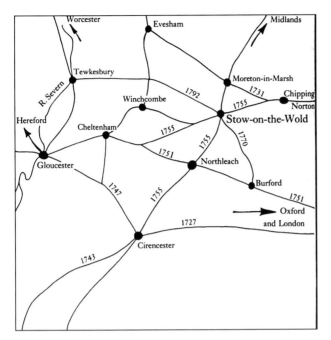

Map showing turnpike
roads in the north
Cotswolds

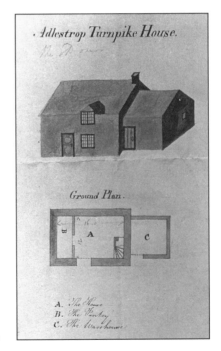

Toll house on the outskirts of Stow

As a local shopping and business centre Stow now had a more varied appearance than formerly. The population rose to over a thousand during the eighteenth century, and was composed of traders, craftsmen and people offering professional services, with farmers still predominating in Maugersbury. Buildings around the Square and in the approaches to it were a mixture of dignified town dwellings, houses with frontages converted into shop premises (Church Street became narrower as front extensions were added to houses there) together with inns and posting houses. Local residents now looked to the shops (as opposed to the markets) to supply their basic household needs, and there was an infinite variety of them. For food, there were butchers, bakers, wine and spirit merchants, and grocers able to supply spices, sugar, dried and candied fruit, preserves, tea, coffee and chocolate. Fruit, vegetables, poultry, dairy produce and fish were still sold at the weekly markets. Other items obtainable were candles, soap, hay, oats and coal – the last an expensive item as turnpike tolls added to the basic cost. We have already noticed that shoes could be bought and repaired, also gloves, saddlery and harness. Haberdashers offered a wide range of materials, trimmings and millinery, and two of them were also undertakers. Dressmakers, tailors and stocking knitters were kept busy with orders from townsfolk and local gentry; a hairdresser refurbished wigs as well as barbering and shaving; paper, ink and sealing wax came from a printer and stationer; and a chemist supplied lavender and rose water, medicines, ointments, 'toothpicks, brushes and dragons' root for the teeth'. Much of the information we have about the shops in Stow comes from the household accounts of local families such as the Leighs and Chamberlaynes. For special clothes, jewellery, plate and furnishings they patronized dealers in London, but household and estate supplies were obtained locally, as were clothes for the children and servants. This interdependence of town traders and craftsmen and their gentry patrons mirrors the link between tenants and overlords in feudal times.

Bill-head of a Stow draper who also acted as an undertaker

St Edward's, a dignified town house in the Square

In addition to goods, Stow also provided services. The fairs had always been and still continued to be occasions when labourers and domestic servants could be found and hired; and at any time, chambermaids, dairymaids, washmaids and lads to help in the garden and stables might be found among the poorer families, since two charities existed to pay for the teaching and training of poor children to enable them to find work in due course. Living in Stow and serving surrounding villages as well were a cow-leech, surgeons and physicians. Among the latter were the Comperes, who first appeared in the seventeenth century and quickly built up a successful practice, which they kept in the family for three generations. They acquired a large estate for themselves through opportune marriages and were accepted socially by the local gentry. Work connected with enclosures and the making of turnpikes called for surveyors, valuers and solicitors, and all these were available, the better-known inns offering suitable accommodation for business meetings and discussions. The making of inventories and valuation of property and goods also required professional handling as did the drawing up of wills and wording of marriage contracts. Land and property owners at the time had a passion for tying things up legally, and though any matter involving a large amount of money might be referred to London lawyers in due course, much of the initial spade work would be done locally.

Serious business was only one aspect of life. Equally important during the eighteenth century were leisure activities, many of which were connected with the inns. Previously these had increased in number to meet the demands of visitors on market days and during the fairs; now the expansion of passenger and goods traffic as a result of the turnpiking of the roads provided a further stimulus. The exact number of inns at any one time is difficult to determine as some came and went rather rapidly, but several of the present establishments were in existence then: the King's Arms, the Unicorn, the White Hart, the Old Red Lion (now the Old Stocks), the Queen's Head and the Talbot. All these offered overnight accommodation for travellers, stabling and post-horse services; the arched entrances of the Unicorn, the White Hart and the King's Arms clearly allowed for the passage of coaches. Both private travellers and users of the stage coaches were catered for, and some of the inns were regular stopping places on the coach and carrier routes where passengers and goods could be picked up or set down. The number of horses needed, men to look after them and smiths and saddlers to deal with urgent repairs must have been considerable; and for those without special skills but willing to frequent inn yards, the chances of odd jobs were greater now than ever before.

As well as for travellers, the inns were a rendezvous for local people, who expected to find some of their pleasures there. Rooms for club meetings, card

Stable yard of the King's Arms, which in the
past accommodated horses, coaches and wagons

parties, musical entertainments and dancing were available; while outside
there were bowling greens, archery butts and skittle alleys for the energetic,
lawns for gentle strolls, and summer houses for resting in the shade. For those
who had means and leisure, local inns served a similar purpose to London
coffee houses, having their regular patrons who met to exchange news,
discuss politics and pick up letters and packages delivered by mail coaches and
carrier services. Card playing also seems to have been a feature of these
informal gatherings to judge by the frequent entries in personal accounts –
mostly of losses. On market days and at fair times, numbers using the public
rooms at the inns were swelled by farmers and traders wanting somewhere
more private than the market place to do business, or ready to seal the
completion of a contract with a drink.

Fairs were still occasions for taking a holiday and enjoying oneself, and
townsfolk of all classes and the neighbouring gentry regularly allowed money
for fairings in their personal finances. Visits of morris dancers and mummers
and May Day festivities were popular entertainments and would end with
thirsty performers and excited spectators all repairing to the inns to celebrate;
also Stow people made up parties to seek amusement elsewhere – race
meetings at Bibury or Tetbury, or Dover's Games at Chipping Campden –
local innkeepers often providing horses and means of transport for the outing.

The Unicorn Hotel, an important coaching inn and social centre for the area

Occasions such as the sovereign's birthday, a military victory or the signing of a peace treaty were celebrated by special peals of bells. Bell-ringing was popular in this area and teams from local villages as well as from Stow would travel round, visiting churches with good bells to be rung. Stow church had a peal of six bells at this time, the upkeep of which was expensive and had to be met by a special levy on the parish.

Some of the travellers passing through Stow and using its inns would have been members of the fashionable élite making for the spas at Bath or Cheltenham in search of relief from chronic illnesses, or the general malaise and weariness engendered by the rigours of the London season, which in fact seems to have been not much more demanding than the routine of 'taking the waters'. The attraction and obvious financial success of Bath, and the marked increase in Cheltenham's prosperity after George III and his family patronized the wells there in 1788, seemed to indicate that any place possessing a mineral spring and some basic amenities might turn itself into a spa; so the discovery of chalybeate in the spring at Lower Swell, together with the traditionally known healing qualities of the water in St Edward's Well, encouraged the people in Stow to try to develop a spa of their own.

What we know about the spa at Stow is largely contained in a poem written in the early nineteenth century called 'The Stow Mineral', seemingly intended as a paeon of praise for what had already been achieved, though

Spa Cottage, site of the potential spa at Stow

there is a hint of subliminal advertising in it also. St Edward's Well was believed to be a source of relief for people with eye trouble; and the spring at Lower Swell might cure rheumatic pain when other medicines had failed. Cases of consumption also benefited from a combination of Stow air and Stow mineral water and the poet would have you believe that many sufferers were dragged back from the brink of death by treatment at the spring. In the attempt to emulate Bath and Cheltenham, a pump room was built at Swell with another cottage beside it where invalids could be looked after; the water could be drunk here on the spot or carried away in bottles, reputedly a lively source of trade. At St Edward's Well there was a cold bath with two ornately decorated houses nearby for rest and refreshment; the approach was by an avenue, running parallel with the Fosse Way between steep, tree-lined banks and under the arched bridge carrying the road to Maugersbury. For those who wanted peace and privacy it afforded a sheltered, secluded walk through a well laid-out pleasure garden aptly named the Retreat.

The urban amenities of Stow, it was believed, were such as would appeal to the sophisticated tastes of those who habitually frequented spas. The inns emphasized the fitness of their rooms, larders and cellars for the entertainment of 'the Quality'; private lodgings were available also, 'well furnished and prepared with speed and ready air'd for every invalid'. The variety of shops has already been noticed, and another feature – typical of a spa – was Archer's lending library, where a selection of histories, plays and novels were available at modest charges, bound in single volumes, convenient for carrying and handling, not too daunting for those in search of undemanding diversion. Should town life become wearisome and pall, Stow could offer in its rural surroundings the simpler pleasures of Arcady – 'a second Eden, sweet and fair'. We are presented with a picture basically idealistic rather than a reality, for in spite of deliberate planning and effort, Stow never achieved the status of a spa. Perhaps it was too near the already successful resorts of Bath and Cheltenham; certainly it lacked the room and means to provide spacious meeting-places and professional entertainments such as these could offer, an eminent doctor to publicize its cures, and royal patronage to add a lustrous veneer to its image.

The eighteenth century ended on a less cheerful note than it had begun. The economic advances made during the period had improved the means and living standards of many people, but there was a reverse side to the picture

Daylesford House, built by Stow workmen for Warren Hastings

which showed others in rapidly worsening circumstances and administrative problems of an unprecedented size and complexity facing the central government and local officials. This situation was complicated even further in the 1790s and early nineteenth century by the consequences of the wars against revolutionary France and Napoleon. Stow did not have such acute social problems as the more industrialized areas of the county, but it did feel the effects of hostilities when taxes on land, houses and windows were increased and indirect taxes on 'luxuries' such as hair powder, servants and dogs were introduced. People of only moderate means were not subjected to all of these, but because Stow was a rural area it was usual for a man to own a horse or a dog, and modernized town houses had their full quota of windows, so almost everyone was affected in some way by wartime exigencies.

In spite of the demands on their purses, the townsfolk of Stow were stirred by patriotic fervour, and not content with sending their usual quota of men to the militia, they decided to raise a troop of cavalry to be known as 'The Cotswold Volunteers'. It consisted of eighty men drawn from Stow, Moreton, Chipping Campden and Northleach, and over £1,000 was raised from these places to cover the expenses of the troop; the womenfolk of the Stow Volunteers sewed a silk standard which was duly dedicated and presented to them. The open spaces round Stow were used for twice-weekly drilling and musketry practice, and though they were not called upon to take any active part in the war the Volunteers kept up their training throughout, and when disbanded gave the money saved from their expenses to the Gloucester Royal Infirmary.

CHAPTER FIVE

Problems of the Nineteenth Century and Their Solutions

The long period of war between 1793 and 1815 had the effect of suspending the normal routine of life and obliging people to accept hardship and difficulties, which, it was hoped, would come to an end with the hostilities that had caused them. However, peace did not bring the expected return to stability. Disturbing trends and problems, already existing before the end of the eighteenth century, began to assume proportions that necessitated the central government stepping in to take responsibility for matters previously left in the hands of local authorities.

Both nationally and locally, the oldest and greatest problem was that of poverty. In a rural area like Stow this was not as widespread as it might have been, but it was on the increase and by the end of the eighteenth century two

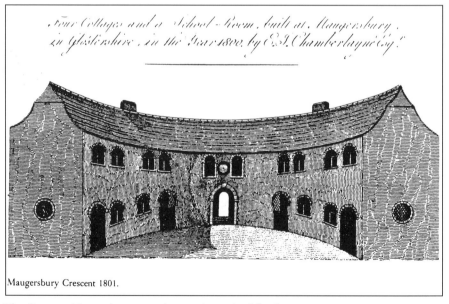

Maugersbury Crescent 1801.

The Crescent, Maugersbury, an early experiment in philanthropy

Friendly Societies had been established in the town, with funds accumulated through subscriptions, available to help members in temporary need or distress. Also, for the duration of the war, a School of Industry was set up to absorb young people and the unemployed and keep them at a useful trade, much of the necessary money and materials being supplied by generous parishioners. At Maugersbury in 1800 Edmund Chamberlayne started a scheme to house some of his poorer tenants decently and enable them to be self-sufficient. This philanthropic experiment was The Crescent, a row of four cottages with a central block consisting of a large room designed to be used as a Sunday school, and underneath, a public oven, a furnace and a coal store. Each cottage was to have an acre of garden and each cottager a pig.

In spite of these efforts, demands for help from the Poor Rate increased and during the 1820s necessitated special meetings of the Parish Council to consider ways of dealing with them. As in the past, the main aim of relief was to underline the shame of poverty rather than rouse sympathy for it, so the Council resorted to putting up notices in public houses listing the names of paupers and parents of illegitimate children who had received sums of money. They even paid for one man and his family to go to America to settle, on condition that they never returned to become a charge upon Stow rates. Then in 1834, with the passing of the Poor Law Amendment Act by Parliament to deal with what was now an acute national problem, Stow was obliged to fall into line with the rest of the country, ceasing to give help to any kind of people living in their own homes, and instead providing a Workhouse where the needy had to go if they wanted public aid. Land was purchased in 1836 and estimates invited from local firms to undertake the work. One for £2,738 was finally accepted from Messrs Clifford and Blizard, who used local stone and local craftsmen to complete the building during the next three years.

Thanks to a succession of kindly Masters, the Stow Union Workhouse never became one of the hated 'Bastilles' of the nineteenth century; nevertheless such institutionalized aid took no account of individual persons or circumstances and everyone who entered the Workhouse had to abide by its rules: men being segregated from the women and children who had to wear a distinctive uniform, and everyone having to accept the monotonous diet and daily routine with an obligation to undertake whatever work they were asked to perform. The women made clothes and did knitting and mending for the inmates, the able-bodied men would be required to take on any casual labour that cropped up such as farm work, stone breaking and quarrying, and road mending.

Another matter of concern was that of public health. In the past all illnesses had been accepted as acts of God and therefore unavoidable, but increasing

The Master's Lodging at Stow Union Workhouse, built 1836–9

medical and scientific knowledge in the seventeenth and eighteenth centuries made people aware that in some cases the causes of disease were discernible and ought to be dealt with. Looking back, we are inclined to blame polluted water supplies and faulty sewerage for much of the ill-health that prevailed, and in the case of Stow this may well have been true. Because of its elevated position on a layer of limestone rock, the town always had a problem with water supplies. Early settlers used the springs on the side of the hill and for a rural community this supply was adequate; but when an urban community began to develop round the market at the top of the hill, water became a problem as it now had to be carried uphill from its source. Though it was a continually running spring, St Edward's Well was not used as much as the wells on the north side of Stow, which were somewhat nearer to the town centre and whence the women carried water in wooden pails attached to yokes over their shoulders. These were the old Roman wells and were shared, not very amicably, with some of the people of Broadwell who claimed to have a prior right to them.

Disputes over the way in which the wells were used and the expense of keeping them in good repair persuaded the townsfolk of Stow to look for other means of securing a regular water supply. At first carts were used to bring water from the spring at Lower Swell and those who could afford it

Water cart at the old Roman well

Water mill at Upper Swell which was used to increase Stow's water supply

Water tower erected in 1867

bought the water at their doors; then an experiment was tried using a windmill at Lower Swell to force water up to Stow through a series of wooden pipes. When this failed, a water wheel was installed at Upper Swell to produce power to provide supplies from there. This, too, proved a failure, and in the middle of the century the poor were still carrying their own water from the wells while carts were bringing supplies for those prepared to buy. By this time Public Health Acts were making it incumbent on local authorities to ensure a regular supply of pure water in their area, so in 1867 the Parish Council ordered a well to be sunk and had a water tower erected over it, and this plan was then improved on, thanks to the generosity of Joseph Chamberlayne who gave £2,000 to the town so that a deeper well could be sunk and a proper system of supply arranged. To mark this advance and record the town's appreciation of such a generous gesture, the old market cross was restored and its present gabled cross added, as a bronze plaque on its side records. The drinking fountain and horse trough replacing the horse pond at the end of High Street with the Fosse Way were further advantages of the new water supply.

Until 1958 sewerage in Stow remained primitive. The town's foundation rock, being limestone, had rain-worn cavities in it which formed natural soakaways under the buildings and obviated the need for a planned drainage system. To what extent the Swillies, as they were called, led to the pollution of local springs, it is impossible to judge; and there is no proof that it was a lack of proper sewerage that caused two serious outbreaks of smallpox in the town in 1833 and 1852, though on each occasion the centre of infection was in the area on the south side of Park Street where slum conditions were said to prevail, prompting the local Board of Health to order heaps of manure and other potential sources of infection to be cleared from the streets, every infected house to be lime-washed, and all communications with the rest of the town to cease except through appointed messengers. So concerned were the members of the Board to safeguard the town's trade and business that once the epidemics were over, they inserted advertisements in local newspapers stating that 'the place could now be revisited by any person with the most perfect safety'.

A third sphere in which local authorities during the nineteenth century were obliged to follow national policy was that of maintaining law and order, since all crimes – in particular theft and assault – were increasing in proportion to the growth of population and spread of social unrest, until they

Fountain on the site of an earlier horse pond at the junction of the High Street and Fosse Way

reached unprecedented limits and demanded attention at a national level. In the past the remedy for a worsening crime rate had been stiffer sentences, but during the 1820s the Home Secretary Robert Peel decided to try a different remedy by adjusting the severity of the punishment to the nature of the offence. He then introduced a scheme to forestall crime, namely the Metropolitan Police Force, which other localities in due course were to copy.

The number and nature of crimes committed in Stow and its neighbourhood did not change much during the early years of the nineteenth century, perhaps because market days and fair times had always given rise to a certain amount of gambling, thieving, drunkenness and fighting, with which the authorities were used to coping. The people of Stow, however, were particularly sensitive to any potential threat to their trade and prosperity, and the safety of those who did business in the town. So the murder in 1834 of a well-respected citizen, an accountant at the Stow Provident Bank, caused an unprecedented public outcry and led, two months later, to the passing of a resolution by the Parish Council 'that a sum of £10 be appropriated for establishing a police constable'. Any doubts as to the expediency of adding more than a penny in the pound to the rates for this purpose were soon dispelled when the first man to hold the post – Police Constable Otway – provided good service to the town and was commended by the Assize Judges

Mr C.S. Whitmore of Lower Slaughter, a generous supporter of Stow activities

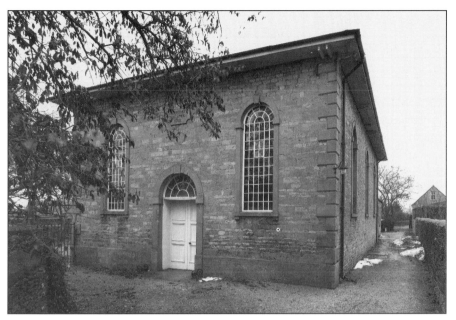

Baptist chapel built in 1852 behind the Manse on Sheep Street

at Gloucester for his conscientiousness. This encouraged people in Stow to subscribe to a fund enabling their constable to maintain the same standard of appearance and deportment as obtained throughout the country. (An order of 1841 directed constables to wear old articles of uniform on night duty and wet days and keep new ones for fine days; they were also warned against being seen with their hair and whiskers in a long and disgusting state.)

As yet there was no police station in Stow and the Justices of the Peace continued to use rooms in the local inns for conducting local business and presiding over the Petty Sessions. These took place at the Unicorn throughout the middle years of the century and frequently provided entertainment for as many townsfolk as could crowd into the court room. By the end of the century a Police Station and Sessions Court had been built at the northern end of the Square, with accommodation for a permanent police presence in the town and suitable facilities for court procedures. It is interesting to note that the severity of the law held no terrors for those outside its clutches. When serious cases were referred from the Petty Sessions to the Assizes, crowds of people from Stow trudged as far as Gloucester to await the outcome and watch public executions should these ensue.

To some nineteenth-century reformers the cure for most evils – whether poverty, disease, unemployment or lawlessness – lay in the provision of education for the masses, which is why this, too, became a matter of national concern wherein local authorities were no longer left free to do what they pleased. In Stow there was the Grammar School of Shepham's foundation, and separate charities provided for the education of a few poor children and the apprenticing of others. The Baptists had a school of their own from 1735 onwards, run by their minister and financed by bequests; and though this turned into a Sunday school in 1810, it continued to attract a number of children because of its good teachers and a library of over two hundred books. These existing facilities, however, provided for only a small section of the children in Stow because it was still widely accepted, save in prosperous homes, that children should be apprenticed to a trade as young as possible or else go to work on the land. Boys who attended the Grammar School and youngsters of both sexes who attended the five small fee-paying schools, started in the early nineteenth century, belonged to families that did not need them to be earning wages, but there was no provision of any kind of elementary education for families of limited means.

This situation continued until the 1830s when Francis Close, rector of Cheltenham, and Colonel Beale-Browne, both keen educationists, together launched an appeal for funds and established an Infants' School for children between two and six years, who paid a penny weekly in fees. The school won

The Revd R.W. Hippisley, rector of Stow

The National Boys' School on the Oddington Road

immediate support and respect and within a month of opening had enrolled 130 pupils. Then in 1844 the proceeds of Shepham's and Townsend's Charities were transferred to a trust for the establishment of a National School providing elementary education and religious instruction. Cottages in Well Lane maintained by Townsend's Charity were used for the school buildings, and the Grammar School, now superseded, was converted into a dwelling for the master of the new school. From this point onwards, for the next thirty years or so, the fortunes of both schools were largely determined by the behaviour of a new rector of Stow, the Revd R.W. Hippisley, who though genuinely anxious to improve many aspects of life for his parishioners, went about his work in such an aggressive manner as to antagonize those he was trying to help. According to one of his curates 'Mr Hippisley and his people were sadly at variance and engaged in never-ending petty squabbles.'

As a leading trustee of the National School the rector was jealous of the success of the Beale-Browne Infant School and publicly accused it of drawing pupils away from the National School; at the same time he caused the latter to be deprived of a government grant towards expenses by insisting on the children's attendance for a session at church every weekday morning, thus flouting a clause in the 1870 Education Act which gave parents the option of withdrawing their children from religious instruction if they were Non-Conformist. Since an appeal for a voluntary rate to a divided parish would have been useless, the National School continued inadequately funded and equipped until, in 1887, to comply with Board of Education regulations, a School Board was established to manage its affairs. The authority of the trustees and particularly that of the Revd Hippisley was thus superseded and things began to run more smoothly. The capacities of the school were much enhanced when it acquired new buildings at the end of the century, one for girls and infants opposite to the Union Workhouse, and one for boys on the Oddington Road, this site having been given for the purpose by Henry Ingles Chamberlayne. Meanwhile the Beale-Browne Infant School, finding it difficult to compete with a government-aided establishment, closed down in 1908, its site being used for the present Roman Catholic church.

Not everything that happened in nineteenth-century Stow was in response to governmental demands. Local enterprise and initiative still operated and were behind some of the innovations which improved public services in the town such as, for instance, the Stow Provident Bank started in 1816, the Post Office started in 1839 and the Stow Gas and Coke Company which after 1860 afforded means of lighting and heating to the town. The Fire Brigade, established in 1874, was another voluntary effort with a fire engine, equipment and fire station bought with subscriptions raised locally, and twenty volunteer firemen enrolled to serve. The rector was asked that one of the church bells might be rung as a fire warning, but his agreement to this

Enoch's Tower, built in 1848 to house a private museum

Stow Fire Brigade, established in 1874 and maintained by voluntary subscriptions

was so hedged in with provisos that it seemed more practicable to have a specific alarm bell. This was hung in a specially built bell-tower in front of St Edward's Hall. The Hall itself, built in 1877–8, was also the result of local enterprise. The funds for it came from the trustees of the Stow Provident Bank, which in 1861 transferred its business to the Post Office Savings Bank but was left with a large amount of unclaimed capital. This the trustees decided to use for the benefit of the town, and so having purchased some buildings in the centre of the Square (a shop and dwellings that had grown out of temporary market erections) they had these destroyed and the Hall built in their place. This quickly became a centre for most of the town's activities. In due course it also afforded a meeting place for the Stow Book Society and room for its considerable collection of books; the contents and furniture of Archer's Lending Library and Reading Room were moved there and put to public use; and the archaeological collection of the Revd David Royce of Lower Swell was deposited there and became the nucleus of the Stow Museum.

Other beneficiaries of local enterprise and generosity were the town's churches. The parish church of St Edward continued to serve the majority of the population in spite of the stormy rectorate of the Revd Hippisley from 1844 to 1898, receiving donations from humble townsfolk as well as the local gentry whenever appeals were launched for repairs to the fabric of the

St Edward's Hall, the centre of the town's activities since it was built in 1877

building and for innovatory improvements. During the course of the century the roof of both aisles and the nave were restored and the whole church repewed; heating and gaslighting were introduced and almost all the windows replaced with contemporary stained glass; a vestry was added and new organ installed in place of the barrel organ which had hitherto been used. The latter had been played or rather turned by one of the almshouse tenants Hailes Parrish, a well-known figure in the town, said to be quite unable to read a note of music. The picture of the Crucifixion by Gaspar de Craeyer, which now hangs at the west end of the church, was presented in 1838 by Joseph Chamberlayne and not long after this Mrs Hippisley, the rector's mother, gave the present clock with its distinctive chime; finally, to celebrate the Diamond Jubilee, two new bells were added to the existing peal of six. During the course of the century a wall was built round the churchyard, giving the whole area a compact unity which it had not had before, and necessitating a more

Hailes Parrish who turned the barrel organ for church services

Church interior (the picture of the Crucifixion is now at the west end)

extensive burial ground being acquired on the outskirts of the town east of the Fosse Way.

At the beginning of the nineteenth century the Baptists already had a chapel and a Sunday school; continued wide support enabled them in 1852 to rebuild the chapel and enhance its approach through an archway on Sheep Street next to the Manse, which was refurbished and modernized at much the same time. Methodism in Stow had a rather unpromising start. John Wesley, who visited the town in 1767 commented: 'I preached at Stow to a very dull, quiet congregation', but seemingly he made an impression on his listeners since a Methodist group was later formed, and within little more than half a century was large enough to finance the building of the present Methodist chapel in the triangle between Sheep Street and Digbeth Street, the land in front of it being given for the planting of a garden by Joseph Chamberlayne. A meeting house and burial ground belonging to the Quakers situated behind the Old Red Lion has disappeared.

Thanks to local firms, Stow's coach and carrier services were extended during the nineteenth century. Previously, the Royal Mail, long distance coaches and carriers had called at Stow and linked the town with key places outside the area. Dawes, a firm operating from Gloucester and Cheltenham, included Stow in its regular 'Fly Waggon' services to London and to all parts of the North. Now

Wesleyan chapel (on the left) before a garden was planted in front of it

Site of Quaker Meeting House and Burial Ground behind the present Old Stocks Hotel

Stow carriers began to operate their own schedules, starting from the inns or their own houses, three each week to London, two to Birmingham, one to Chipping Norton and Cirencester, and daily to Cheltenham; and until the town had its own station there were daily services to Faringdon and to Cheltenham to connect with trains there. Ultimately, in 1881, the completion of the Great Western Cheltenham to Banbury line gave Stow a direct rail link with services to London via Banbury or Cheltenham. For this particular purpose Stow station was never used to any great extent, as the Worcester to London line through Moreton had a halt at Adlestrop, nearly as convenient for Stow people as the town station, which perforce had to be built at the bottom of the hill on the Burford road, and which apart from people making local journeys was primarily useful for the unloading of coal supplies for the Gas Company.

The nineteenth century was not exclusively spent in making administrative progress and improving the amenities of the town. Stow people still had their lighter moments. Fairs and markets as always brought temptation and entertainment in their train. As late as 1822 three men appeared with performing bears in tow, and one of the men displayed himself as 'a natural curiosity' being covered with scaly hide instead of skin and sprouting an abnormal amount of hair. Gambling was on the increase, and officials had to be constantly on the alert for evidence of this, such as dice, cards, marked skins and boards; closed carts, dark places behind stalls and narrow alleys made

Stow station which closed in the 1950s

ideal spots for a quick game of chance, and unpremeditated searches among the most innocent-looking goods often confirmed official suspicions. By the end of the century clubs for many sports existed – cricket, football, quoits, bowling, golf – the Unicorn Inn and its grounds usually providing the necessary facilities for regular meetings and yearly celebrations. Every meeting of the Archery Club was turned into a social occasion, when for a 6s. ticket members might enjoy 'Archery at 12 o'clock; Dinner at 3, Tea at 6, and conclude with Dancing until 9'. For the less athletically inclined, there was a Philharmonic Society founded in 1876, a Choral Society, a Floral and Horticultural Society, and an Agricultural Society formed jointly with Moreton and Chipping Norton.

The long reign of Queen Victoria provided a number of special dates for celebration: the accession, coronation, marriage, births of children and finally the Diamond Jubilee. All these led to holidays, special peals of bells, entertainments and feasts – the latter, along with a distribution of money to the poor, largely supplied by neighbouring gentry. Until the middle of the century there were the usual processions on the patronal day of St Edward, on May Day and at Whitsun; but by the end of the century these had all been run together and replaced by a Club Day when everyone took a holiday, put on their best clothes and enjoyed whatever activities were going on.

Recreation ground at the Unicorn Hotel, used for bowls, archery and other sports

Coronation Day celebrations in Digbeth Street (1911)

Stow Club Day, Park Street

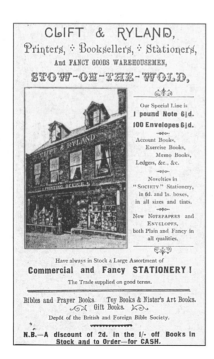

Clift & Ryland, printers and stationers since the eighteenth century

A procession round the town would have been joined by the Stow Volunteer Reserve and the Fire Brigade in uniform, eminent public figures and tradesmen, groups and associations with banners proudly on display, and decorated farm carts. Visiting teams of dancers, bell-ringers and local children provided entertainment, and responsible for background music was the Stow Brass Band which continued to play for dancing well into the night. Until recently there were still people in Stow who claimed that it was the heady atmosphere engendered by Stow Club Day that had led them to propose and subsequently to marry!

For those who wished to keep abreast of all business and social occasions, and to have in hand for easy reference the dates of fairs, Quarter Sessions and Auction Sales, the times and prices of carrier and postal services and even current tax rates, there was a local Year Book produced by the printers Clift

STOW POST OFFICE STAFF, 1913.

Back Row.—J. H. Webb, S. Lockey, J. H. Woodward, L. W. Appleton, J. C. Acock C. Faulkner, C. Hoare, E. Perkins, H. B. Bridges.
Middle Row.—Miss K. M. Ryland, Miss P. R. Gibbs.
Front Row.—Miss F. A. Fisher, Miss A. A. Fisher (postmistress), Miss M. B. Stroud

Post Office staff

POST OFFICE.

Post Mistress—MISS F. M. EATON.

OFFICE HOURS.—Week Days 7 a.m. to 8 p.m.
Sundays 8 a.m. to 10 a.m.
Sale of Stamps, &c., 7 a.m. to 8 p.m. Sundays 8 to 10 a.m.
Savings Bank, Money Order, Government Annuity and Insurance
Business, and Licenses, 8 a.m. to 8 p.m.
Sale and Payment of Postal Orders 7 a.m. to 8 p.m.
Telegraph Business 8 a.m. to 8 p.m. Sundays 8 to 10 a.m.

DELIVERIES.		DESPATCHES.		
The delivery of letters and parcels commence in the Town at		Letter box cleared for despatch at	Parcels for the same despatch accepted until	
Week Days.	Sund's	Week Days.	Sundays.	W'k'd'y only
London, South and General	7 a.m.	10.15 a.m.	5.0 p.m.	10.10 a.m.
North ... 8.15 a.m. 8.15 a.m	6.10 p.m.	Registered Letters accepted up to 10 a.m		
General ... 1.45 p.m	7.15 p.m.		7.0 p.m

For registered Letters 15 minutes earlier for each despatch.

☞ NO DELIVERY OF PARCELS ON SUNDAYS.

—: POSTMEN. :—

		LEAVES.		SUNDAYS.
		a.m.	p.m.	a.m.
TOWN	A. E. Jefferies	8.15	1.45	8.15
Broadwell & Donnington	John King	8.15	..	8.15
Maugersbury & Icomb	E. Perkins	8.15		Maug. only
Wyck Rissington ..	H. Hicks ..	8.15		
Oddington	W. Richings	8.15	1.45	..
Upper Swell & Condicote	L. Clifford	8.15		..
Lower Swell	J. C. Acocks	7.0	2.45	8.15

WALL BOXES CLEARED AT

Donnington 5.20 p.m. Broadwell S.O. 5.40 p.m. Sundays 10 a.m.
Lower Oddington S.O. 9.25 a.m. and 5.10 p.m. Upper Oddington
9.35 a.m. and 5.20 p.m. Condicote 5.0 p.m. Lower Swell 8.40
a.m. and 5.40 p.m. Sundays 9.35 a.m. Wyck Rissington 4.15 p.m.
Icomb S.O. 5.0 p.m. Maugersbury 5.40 p.m.

Letters posted in Stow before 10.15 a.m. are delivered the same day in
London, Oxford, Evesham, Blockley, Campden, Moreton, Bourton,
Chipping Norton, Birmingham, Witney, Banbury, Cheltenham,
Gloucester, Bicester, Shipston-on-Stour, Reading, Bristol, Worcester,
Stratford-on-Avon

Bill of Postal Services from Clift's Almanack
(1892)

and Ryland, a business long established in the town. The latter also acted as
an agency and distribution centre for a district newspaper, *Moreton Free Press
and Stow-on-the-Wold News*, published every Saturday, price 1d. and well
patronized in both places. Stow people clearly enjoyed everything that went
on in their town and savoured it in retrospect as well.

The nineteenth century saw the modernization of Stow in so far as all
matters connected with local government were gradually taken over by an
Urban District Council, with special committees for Health, Housing,
Highways, and so forth, and all the existing charities of the town were
reorganized into a Parochial Charities Scheme which thereafter distributed
£52 a year to six almspeople living in the houses near the church and spent
any remaining money on fuel and goods for the deserving poor. But, as in
many other places, general remedies did not always solve particular problems,
and it is noticeable right up to the end of the century that gentry benefactors
and enterprising townsfolk still continued to play a significant part in local
affairs. Members of the Chamberlayne, Leigh, Hastings and Whitmore
families, when aware of gaps in official methods of providing for the poor,
were quick to offer supplementary benefits and aid; when anyone was needed
to take the lead in new civic ventures their names headed lists of subscribers

Advertisement for Teague's Foundry

and active helpers; when celebrations were called for, they provided food and drink for dinners, presents for the very young and very old, and gratuities for bell-ringers, musicians and other entertainers. Furthermore, leading craftsmen and traders, for example Clifford, Collett, Hiatt, Hanckes, Blizard (names familiar in local records since the sixteenth century), were prominent among supporters of the parish church and Non-Conformist chapels and provided skilled workmanship when new buildings were being erected or old ones repaired; while among more recent comers to the area, the Teague and Hollis families started an up-to-date iron foundry, and the Arkells their brewery at Donnington, both of which, by employing local labour and using local outlets for their products, made a valuable contribution to the prosperity of the town.

CHAPTER SIX

Stow in the Twentieth Century

The turn of the century made little difference to the old way of life in Stow and it was not until the outbreak of war in 1914 that it effectively came to an end. Up to this point the Thursday market was the high spot of the week, when farmers from the neighbourhood flocked into Stow with their families to buy and sell goods, to do business with the banks, auctioneers and solicitors and end the day convivially at one of the inns. Wheat, barley, cheese, meat and leather goods still predominated among the goods sold, along with agricultural implements and machinery, the latter laid out on display in front of the foundry at the top of Digbeth Street, regardless of inconvenience to passers-by. Twice yearly the fairs continued to attract crowds from near and far; and at normal times the town continued to serve local residents and nearby villages through its useful shops, public services and schools.

By 1918 the situation had changed considerably. Hit by wartime shortages and the deaths of men on active service, many shops and businesses had closed down, and there were noticeably fewer individuals such as dressmakers, milliners and laundresses offering their services. Having been suspended for the duration, the market and Stow Club Day never resumed, and even though the fairs continued, they were for amusement only except for the sale of livestock, saddlery and farming equipment on Horse Fair days. During the 1920s and 1930s, as motorized traffic gradually replaced horses and horse-drawn vehicles, the demand for smiths, carters and stablemen declined and the opening of garages on the approach roads to Stow by no means compensated for the loss of employment in trades that had been traditional in the town for centuries. The closing of the Elms Private School after more than half a century was another pointer to declining prosperity in the town.

The outbreak of a second war in this century once more disrupted normal life in Stow, and when hostilities ended there were fewer openings for making the kind of living that most people now expected, which led many residents in the town to seek work elsewhere. Moreover, thanks to the expansion of tourism in the area, shops and services catering for visitors began to proliferate at the expense of providing basic necessities for local people. Thus,

Amusement fair in the Square

An early twentieth-century shop front

Playground behind the Elms School in the corner of the Square

One of the garages opened between the wars. The site is now occupied by new housing

in addition to those going further afield to work, as many as had cars or could use local bus services began to go to larger places, offering entertainments, supermarkets and chain stores to satisfy household and personal needs. According to people who lived in Stow during the 1950s and 1960s, in spite of its growing population (increased from about 1,200 to 1,700 in the first half of the century), the town appeared to be in decline, lacking a sense of purpose and future prospects.

Since then, however, the situation has changed somewhat, and instead of relying on its traditional role as a market centre for the area, Stow is seeking to bolster its prosperity by other means. Primarily its hopes are pinned on the steady stream of visitors to the place, not just at the height of the holiday season but more or less throughout the year, for whom it is accustomed and has the capacity to cater. Many of the hotels that offer food and shelter to travellers are those that did so in the past, and there are newer establishments as well as private houses offering accommodation. No less important is the Youth Hostel, one of the first to be established in Britain, which in the course

Stow Lodge, the Old Rectory, is now a hotel

Sezincote, the Mogul architecture of which is said to have inspired the Prince Regent's plans for his Pavilion at Brighton

of a year has as many as seven thousand visitors from countries all over the world. Two new shopping precincts built on historic sites in the town – at the rear of the Talbot Hotel and in the old Brewery Yard – are of interest to holiday-makers, while the many antique shops and art galleries attract foreign as well as English dealers and collectors here on business. For these, and for visitors anxious to explore the Cotswold area to the full, Stow makes a convenient stopping-place and a centre for touring, being within easy reach of other popular resorts such as Broadway and Bourton-on-the-Water, many attractive Cotswold villages, the historical sites of Chedworth Roman Villa, Sudeley Castle and Sezincote, and the well-known gardens of Hidcote, Batsford and Abbotswood.

Fair days, as in the past, continue to attract visitors from a wide area though their character is changing and their popularity is causing unprecedented problems. The auctioning of horses, perhaps the most important feature of the fairs since the seventeenth century, now takes place at Andersford, still

The old style Horse fair

The Horse fair: modern overflow from the Square

carefully organized by Tayler and Fletcher, a firm that has been handling such sales in the area for over a century. Meanwhile the entertainments and sideshows customarily based in the Square, have been outnumbered by the stalls set up on the verges of the approach roads to Stow, selling a miscellaneous range of goods including horses, but without the controls that formerly applied, and causing such serious congestion as to detract from the pleasure of the occasion. History would appear to be repeating itself! In 1664 Edmund Chamberlayne, lord of the manor, pondered taking legal action against those 'att my fayre att Stowe that lye out with their cheese and corn – and so keepe a fayre without the towne'.

As well as on fair days, Stow can exploit its traditional past in other ways. Its open Square and stone-built houses, its old inns and narrow streets all lend themselves as suitable settings for films, and it is surprising how convincingly the past can be restored by a layer of peat on the road and the masking of shop and road signs. Places nearby have also been used for film-making, with Stow townsfolk providing extras and much of the accommodation and services needed by production units.

On two other occasions recently the town has successfully planned and coped with mass incursions of visitors. In 1976 it celebrated the

A picturesque corner of the Square

Morris dancing, traditional in the north Cotswolds

quincentenary of its second charter fair and during the summer season, through the concerted efforts of residents, re-created some of the past. The Square was cleared of traffic to make way for a medieval market; peals of bells were rung by the Stow ringers and visiting teams; the wells were dressed in traditional fashion; and troupes of morris dancers came from round about to perform some of the sequences indigenous to the area, for example Bledington 'Balance the Straw', Longborough 'Old Truckle' and Oddington 'Swaggering Boney'. These were a reminder that this part of the Cotswolds was the traditional home of morris dancing and its accompanying music, and that Cecil Sharp and others who in this century have tried to record information about the custom were given considerable help by Stow dancers and fiddlers. The Quincentenary Exhibition, illustrating five hundred years of the town's history, brought to light a wealth of valuable material from the past: whole collections of craftsmen's tools; bonnets and aprons worn by the Workhouse inmates; shepherd's smocks; farm implements; examples of work from the silk mills at Blockley; the church plate, most of it given by the Chamberlayne family; and the traditional standard weights and measures put to unusual use by Admiral Chamberlayne in 1830 to get him a place at the coronation of William IV, when he carried them up the aisle of Westminster Abbey shouting 'Make way for the weights and measures of Maugersbury.'

Chalice (dated 1682) from the collection of church plate, most of it given by the Chamberlayne family

In July 1992 members of the Sealed Knot set up camp in fields on the outskirts of Stow, in preparation for re-enacting the battle fought in 1646. A typical Cotswold drizzle prevailed during the weekend giving the modern fighters a taste of what their forebears endured while engaged in the Civil Wars. Once again the Fosse Way echoed to the sounds of marching feet and clanking weaponry; the Square was crowded with soldiery; and the townsfolk provided accommodation and hospitality for spectators and combatants alike – no doubt with considerable more readiness than local residents greeted incursors in the 1640s.

While successfully coping with and catering for its ever increasing number of visitors, it is not so easy for Stow to comply with Gloucestershire's plan for its promotion as a centre for employment opportunities. The town can offer only a limited number of openings in connection with tourism and the services needed in the surrounding area, so there is a tendency for the young to seek opportunities elsewhere. As a result the average age of Stow dwellers is getting higher, and although since 1918 several estates of family homes have been built on the eastern side of the town, and there has been infilling in the town itself as well, the chief demand is for retirement homes and accommodation for the elderly such as is already being provided at Ashton House, Chamberlayne House and Reynolds Homes.

Allotments at the rear of East View (formerly Stow Union Workhouse) where residents grew their own vegetables

Reynolds Homes, founded to provide accommodation for elderly Stow residents

However, although it has a large elderly element in its population, the town of Stow does not lack energy and resilience. The Chamber of Commerce and the Stow and District Civic Society watch assiduously over its business interests, amenities and the conservation of its buildings and history. There are a number of clubs and societies that cater for the athletic, artistic and musical interests of its residents. The annual Summer Fête is as enthusiastically supported as the Stow Club Day was in the past; and scarcely a weekend goes by without a sale in aid of charity, or some other event being held in the Square, in St Edward's Hall or the Church Room. Should there be an urgent need for action to be taken over a particular issue, volunteers are never lacking, as was demonstrated recently in respect of a pedestrian crossing in Park Street.

In January 1990 the people of Stow were shocked when gales destroyed many of the beech trees that lined the Fosse Way on Stow Hill, and with them a well-known and very striking approach to the town. However, this was regarded as a challenge to be met, not just ignored. A Committee of the Civic Society was set up to organize fund-raising and conscript active help in clearing the verges, removing dead stumps, repairing fallen walls and ultimately replacing the lost trees. Thanks to tireless individual efforts and contributions from local businesses and the Countryside Commission,

Beech trees lining the approach to Stow before the storms

Gaps in trees after the storms. The survivors are highlighted by frost

Children planting young beeches

Stow's spacious market square overlooked by the church

enough money was raised in two years for paid work to be started, though some of the initial clearing and stone-walling had already been done voluntarily. Meanwhile, children at Stow Primary School were given beech seedlings to set and tend; and when the ground had been prepared, these were planted and each child given a certificate to mark the event. With beech trees that were donated and the seedlings grown by the children, a thousand trees in all were planted along the Fosse by the summer of 1993 – surely proof of an enduring community spirit in the town.

Although on a summer's day when the Square is packed with cars and sightseers Stow closely resembles other Cotswold resorts, it nevertheless retains some unique characteristics. Travellers approaching the town from whatever direction will have seen the church tower from afar and will have had to climb the hill that in early days was the chief protection of the community living there. Even ranks of parked cars cannot conceal the spaciousness of the Square that so easily accommodated markets and fairs, nor the dominance of the church, still overlooking the town's activities, and as in the past, the responsibility of the parishioners to maintain. Only a short walk away from the town centre lies Maugersbury, still a rural community, with fields and meadows where, by custom, rushes were cut for use in Stow church; St Edward's Well, its spiritual qualities now forgotten; the remains of woods that provided shelter, building material and fuel for the first settlers in

Aerial view of present day Stow, still shaped by its roads and dominated by its church

The Unicorn Crossing. Four streams of traffic now dominate the former quiet venue of the Heythrop Hunt

the area; and farms that started out as feudal holdings and achieved their present size and names during the prosperous years of the eighteenth century.

Stow's past continues to exist and thrive along with its present, which may be its future too, as long as the town continues to offer the kind of services that travellers have needed ever since the first traders and pilgrims ventured along the old tracks that converged on the hilltop at Stow; for above all else, it is the roads that throughout Stow's history have determined the size, character and fortunes of the community living here.

Bibliography

ORIGINAL SOURCES

Gloucester Record Office, Stow-on-the-Wold, D 149/D 610/P317.
Shakespeare Birthplace Trust, Stoneleigh MSS, Adlestrop Papers, Maugersbury Manorial Records.
Worcester Record Office, Evesham Abbey Court Book.

SECONDARY SOURCES

Victoria County History, Volume VI.
Brill, Edith, *Life and Tradition in the Cotswolds* (1973).
Finberg, Jocelyn, *The Cotswolds* (1977).
Johnson, Joan, *Stow-on-the-Wold* (1980).
Rudder, Samuel, *A New History of Gloucestershire* (1779).
Rudge, Thomas, *The Agriculture of Gloucestershire* (1789).
Smith, Brian, *The Cotswolds* (1992).
Witts, F.E., *Diary of a Cotswold Parson*.

Acknowledgements

For this revised edition of my previous book on Stow, I am indebted to those residents who have given me up-to-date information for Chapter Six. I also wish to thank the following for providing photographs and granting permission for their reproduction, in particular Bob Sharp who made the whole of his unique collection available to me: Mrs M. Checketts (85a), Cheltenham Museum and Art Gallery (2), Mrs M. Hedges (76a), Anthony Kersting (31, 37), Dr Michael King (85b), Oxford City Library (3, 49, 65b), Royal Commission on Historical Monuments (42, 59, 77, 82), Mrs B. Ruddock (36), Shakespeare Birthplace Trust (14, 43, 44), Bob Sharp (9, 13, 20, 24, 25, 27, 45, 47, 48, 54, 55a, 56, 57, 60, 61, 62, 63, 64, 65a, 67, 68, 69, 70a, 71, 75, 76b, 79, 81, 88), Society for the Protection of Ancient Monuments (55), William Walker (19, 33, 41), Mrs P. Whitmore (58).

I travelled one day thro' the rain and the cold,
From the gay streets of London to Stow-on-the-Wold,
And I sighed to myself, 'twill be dreary and cold,
A regular desert at Stow-on-the-Wold.
But a sweet little couple I happened to meet,
Trudging on hand in hand, down the long village street,
And I own that it <u>need</u> not be dreary or cold,
At the veriest desert like Stow-on-the-Wold.

from the *Illustrated Children's Birthday Book*
(ed. F.E. Weatherly)

Index

(Illustrations in italics)